User's Guide to
the Bible

User's Guide to the Bible

STEPHEN M. MILLER

A Lion Book
an imprint of
Lion Hudson plc
Mayfield House, 256 Banbury Road,
Oxford OX2 7DH, England
www.lionhudson.com
ISBN 0 7459 5196 1

First edition 2006
10 9 8 7 6 5 4 3 2 1 0

A catalogue record for this book is available
from the British Library

Typeset in 12/13 Lapidary333
Printed and bound in Singapore

Contents

Introduction

If you've ever taken a trip to unfamiliar territory, you know the value of a guidebook. Without one, you wouldn't know where to start – especially if the territory you're travelling through is huge.

There's no way I would venture into another country without first reading up on it and learning about highlights, things to watch out for and wonderful sights I wouldn't want to miss.

That's what *User's Guide to the Bible* is – a guidebook. Oddly, though, it's a guidebook to another book: the Bible. So you might wonder, what's the point? Why not just read the Bible?

Let me give you two reasons.

1. The Bible isn't just one book. It's a library of 66 books, written in many genres by an unknown number of writers over a span of time that stretches well beyond a millennium. So it's hard to know where to start.

2. Also, it was written 2,000–3,000 years ago in an unfamiliar time and culture. As I write this introduction, my son is preparing to take a final exam on *Macbeth*. He is reading the play, but it was written at the same time the *King James Version* of the Bible was being translated and is just about as hard to understand. The setting is different, by some 400 years. The

culture is foreign to him. And the words are incredibly strange. So he's also reading a guide to *Macbeth*, to help him understand the story better.

The Bible is far more complex than *Macbeth* (with apologies to Shakespeare). If ever there was a book that needed a guide to point out highlights, things to watch out for and other tips for reading, it's the Bible.

User's Guide to the Bible gives you a quick synopsis of each of the 66 books in the Bible's library. Each book is summed up in a paragraph, with the key points, main characters, biggest scenes and most famous passages drawn out. There are also concise articles about how God gave us the Bible, the Bible's main message, tips for interpreting what you read and tools to help you study the Bible. You will also learn about famous Bible people and places, and archaeological evidence that supports the Bible. In addition, you will read answers to some of the most frequent questions people ask about Bible stories and teachings.

This isn't, however, a book to replace the Bible. This is a 'John the Baptist' kind of a book that points the way to something much better. When Jewish scholars asked John who he was, he said he was just someone preparing the way for another – a person 'who will soon begin his ministry. I am not even worthy to be his slave' (John 1:27). That person was Jesus.

User's Guide to the Bible is also preparing the way for the Word of God. If we can get you past our book and into his Book – equipped to read it with new insight – we've done our job.

A word of thanks

I'd like to thank the Lion editorial team, Morag Reeve, Catherine Giddings, Jonathan Roberts and Juliet Mozley, along with one other important person, my wife and first-round proofreader, Linda.

Stephen M. Miller

Bible Timeline

Most dates are approximate

Date	Before 2500 BC	2500–2000 BC	2000–1500 BC	1500–1000 BC	1000–500 BC	500–0 BC	AD 0–100
World events	2550: Great Pyramid built at Giza	2000: Babylonian Epic of Gilgamesh, first known written story	1790: Hammurabi's Code with 282 laws – some similar to laws of Moses	1500: Hinduism starts in India 1440: Thutmose III ('Napoleon of Egypt') reigns 1250: Rameses the Great rules Egypt	1000: Phoenicians create alphabet 776: first known Olympics	323: Alexander the Great dies after conquering Middle East 63: Rome takes Jerusalem 7: Saturn and Jupiter align	July 64: two-thirds of Rome burns – Christians blamed 70: Romans destroy Jerusalem and last Jewish temple 79: Mount Vesuvius erupts near Naples
Bible events	Before 4000: Creation Before 2500: Flood	2100s: God promises homeland to Abraham's descendants	1800s: Jacob moves family to Egypt to escape famine; descendants become slaves	1440: (or mid-1200s) Moses leads Hebrew exodus out of Egypt 1035: Israelites crown Saul their first king	931: Israel splits into Israel and Judah 722: Israel falls to Assyria 586: Judah falls to Babylon 538: Jews rebuild Jerusalem	40–4: Herod the Great rules Judea 7–4: Jesus is born	30: Jesus crucified 43: Paul begins ministry to non-Jews 44: Apostle James is first disciple executed 67: Paul executed 90s: John writes last book of Bible, Revelation
Bible people	Before 4000: Adam and Eve Before 2500: Noah	2100s: Abraham 2000s: Isaac	1900s: Jacob 1800s: Joseph	1400s: (or 1200s) Moses 1100s: Samson 1000s: David	900s: Solomon 700s: Isaiah and many other Jewish prophets 600s: Jeremiah and many other Jewish prophets	7–4 BC–AD 30: Jesus	Jesus Peter and disciples Paul
Bible book setting	Genesis	Genesis	Genesis, Exodus, possibly Job	Exodus, Leviticus, Numbers, Deuteronomy, Joshua, Judges, Ruth, 1–2 Samuel	1–2 Kings, 1–2 Chronicles, Song of Songs, most books of prophecy	Esther, Ezra, Nehemiah, Malachi, Matthew, Luke	New Testament

The Bible in one page

God created a perfect world, according to the Bible. But it didn't stay perfect. That's because he gave human beings the freedom to make choices.

Humanity's first couple, Adam and Eve, made a tragic choice. They broke the only law God gave them. They ate forbidden fruit.

Suddenly, everything changed – as though sin had a toxic effect that contaminated creation. Humans, once intimate with God, were now separated from him. The garden paradise became a weed patch, and enduring health gave way to disease and death.

The Bible is the story of God working to reclaim his perfect creation, and to overcome sin and its harmful effects. He starts with one righteous man who is devoted to him: Abraham. From Abraham, God grows a nation that is devoted to him: Israel. And God's plan for these people is that 'You will be a light to guide all nations to me' (Isaiah 42:6).

However, Israel disappoints God by persistently breaking his most basic laws. So God sends prophets to warn them of the disastrous effects that their continued sin will produce. In time, Israel is wiped off the world map. But God restores the nation, and in a miraculous virgin birth he sends his own Son to complete Israel's mission. Jesus teaches people how to live as citizens of God's kingdom. And then, by his execution and resurrection from the dead, Jesus proves that this kingdom is forever.

'Go and make disciples of all nations,' he tells his followers (Matthew 28:19).

God's plan to guide all nations to himself will be accomplished in a new beginning, 'Look,' says John, reporting a vision of this future. 'The home of God is now among his people! He will live with them, and they will be his people. God himself will be with them. He will remove all of their sorrows, and there will be no more death or sorrow or crying or pain. For the old world and its evils are gone forever.' (Revelation 21:3–4)

How God gave us the Bible

Some of the Bible's most famous stories were probably passed along by word of mouth for centuries before anyone bothered to write them down. That was because most people didn't read or write 3,000 years ago; but they all enjoyed hearing stories of their heritage told by older family members and by gifted storytellers in the community.

The first writer the Bible mentions is Moses, who lived in the 1400s BC or the 1200s BC – Bible experts still debate that. Jewish tradition says he wrote the first five books of the Bible, though the books themselves don't say who wrote them.

Yet Moses probably did write down many of the laws preserved in the second to the fifth books of the Bible: Exodus, Leviticus, Numbers, and Deuteronomy. This is a fair assumption, because God told him to 'write down all these instructions, for they represent the terms of my covenant with you and with Israel' (Exodus 34:27). Genesis, however, contains stories from many centuries before Moses.

Bible experts guess that when David became king, palace officials started recording Jewish history – including stories that had been passed along from generation to generation. Four hundred years after David, when invaders wiped the Jewish nation off the map and exiled the survivors to what is now Iraq, the Jews could no longer express their faith by worshipping in Jerusalem and offering sacrifices there. The best they could do was to read their sacred writings as an act of worship. Many Bible experts agree that it was during this time that Jewish scholars finished recording most of the writings of the Old Testament.

It's a mystery how or when the Jews decided which writings were sacred. References in the Bible to different categories of scripture suggest that the first books the Jews embraced as sacred were the opening five books, called the Law. Then came

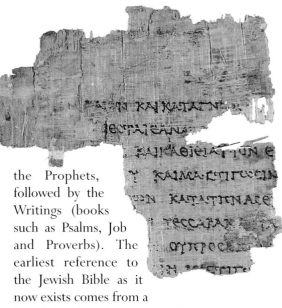

the Prophets, followed by the Writings (books such as Psalms, Job and Proverbs). The earliest reference to the Jewish Bible as it now exists comes from a Jewish book written in the first century AD called 2 Esdras. The entire process of writing, compiling, and accepting the books as sacred probably took over a thousand years. It was much shorter for the New Testament. The books were all written within a few decades, and were quickly and widely embraced. The last book, Revelation, was probably written in the AD 90s.

Surprisingly, stories about Jesus, recorded in the Gospels of Matthew, Mark, Luke, and John, were probably not the first New Testament books written. As long as the disciples were alive to give their eyewitness accounts, most people saw no reason to write the stories down. That came later, when leading disciples began dying as martyrs.

Probably the oldest New Testament book is a letter that the apostle Paul wrote to a church in Thessalonica, a city in what is now Greece. Bible experts say he wrote it around AD 50, some twenty years after Jesus' crucifixion.

Letters by Paul and other church leaders, along with the Gospels and a history of the church (Acts of the Apostles),

Above: From the 100s BC, a fragment of the Septuagint – the world's first Bible translation.

13

were copied and circulated among church congregations. In time, most Christians came to accept them in the same way they accepted the Jewish Bible – a book Paul described this way:

> 'Every part of Scripture is God-breathed and useful one way or another – showing us truth, exposing our rebellion, correcting our mistakes, training us to live God's way. Through the Word we are put together and shaped up for the tasks God has for us.' (2 Timothy 3:16)

Though Paul was talking about the Old Testament, Christians came to recognize this letter, written to his friend Timothy, as part of sacred scripture, too. In fact, Paul's letters in general were described as 'scripture' before the end of the first Christian century: the apostle Peter himself identifies them with 'the rest of the scriptures' in 2 Peter 3:16.

Church leaders eventually affirmed what the church had already been practicing for centuries. At the Council of Carthage in AD 397, they declared the 27 books of the New Testament as a God-inspired addition to the 39 books of the Old Testament.

Why it takes faith
to believe the Bible

Sometimes we don't need faith.

We don't need it to believe we're at the foot of a mountain when we can see the mountain with our own eyes.

And we don't need it to believe that if we walk off a cliff we'll fall, because we've experienced gravity – and some of us have the X-rays to prove it.

But when an ancient book written mainly by unnamed authors tells us about a God we have never seen and a spiritual dimension we have never experienced, a little proof would be quite nice.

There's a problem, however.

No one has figured out how to prove the existence of something spiritual to someone physical. We can't take a tissue sample from God and test his DNA. We can't fly a space shuttle to heaven and photograph the pearly gates.

There are some things we can't prove, and that we have to accept by faith – or reject.

Jesus was a good example of this. He wanted to convince people that he was God's Son, but most never believed him. Even his twelve disciples had trouble. In frustration one day Jesus finally told them, 'At least believe because of what you have seen me do' (John 14:11). They had seen him do many miracles: turn water into wine, walk on water, heal the sick, and even raise the dead. Yet they did not fully believe until they saw the most remarkable signs of all: his death, resurrection and ascension into the heavens.

Even that was not proof Jesus was God's Son. But it was enough for the disciples. They believed.

The Bible presents itself as God's message to human beings. One of the writers puts it this way: 'We saw it with our own eyes: Jesus resplendent with light from God the Father as the voice of Majestic Glory spoke: "This is my Son, marked by my love, focus of all my delight." We were there on the holy mountain with him. We heard the voice out of heaven with our very own ears' (2 Peter 1:16–18).

We can't prove that Peter's words are true – that the message he and others delivered in what became the New Testament was from God. Yet there are many remarkable signs that point us in that direction and which urge us to believe the Bible.

Here are some of those signs:

● **History.** Many discoveries support the Bible's historical accuracy. Roman writers discussed the crucifixion and resurrection of Jesus as well as the execution of John the Baptist. Archaeologists have found documents from Assyria, Babylon and Persia that support Bible accounts of battles and their aftermath. Names of Bible characters – from a scribe called Baruch to a king called David – have shown up on seals and engravings.

● **Prophecy.** Many Old Testament prophecies were fulfilled in New Testament times. Most startling is one prophecy about Jesus, recorded on an Isaiah scroll copied 100 years before Jesus was born and discovered among the famous Dead Sea Scrolls. A section called the Suffering Servant passage sounds like an eyewitness report of Jesus' crucifixion: 'He was wounded and crushed for our sins. He was beaten that we might have peace. He was whipped, and we were healed… who among the people realized that he was dying for their sins… he was buried like a criminal; he was put in a rich man's grave' (Isaiah 53:5–9).

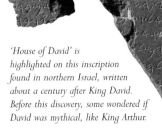

'House of David' is highlighted on this inscription found in northern Israel, written about a century after King David. Before this discovery, some wondered if David was mythical, like King Arthur.

Centuries before the printing press, a monk meticulously copies sacred words onto a page for a new edition of the Holy Bible.

- **Martyrdom.** Prophets and disciples put their lives on the line to deliver the message preserved in the Bible. Most of Jesus' disciples were executed because of what they taught. So were many prophets.

- **Jesus.** His Bible was the Old Testament, and he quoted it often. When Satan tempted him to break his desert fast and turn stones into bread, Jesus quoted from Deuteronomy 8:3, 'No! The Scriptures say, "People need more than bread for their life; they must feed on every word of God"' (Matthew 4:4).

- **Honesty.** The Bible's most basic teachings ring true. God asks us to observe the Ten Commandments, which Jesus summed up in a Golden Rule: treat others the way you want to be treated. Our experience confirms that this is solid advice. We're better off when we treat others with respect and compassion. But when we lie, steal, or murder, we can expect painful consequences.

17

How inspired is the Bible?

The Bible is inspired like no other book in history, many Christians say.

Some insist that God even dictated the words, and that the original manuscripts were flawless. Others say it doesn't matter – we don't have any originals. What matters, they argue, is this: How inspired is the Bible we have today?

'Fully inspired,' most Christians answer. God directed the ancient writers, who used their own style and in some cases added their own observations. And he directed the scribes who made copies of scrolls that started wearing out, though they sometimes made copying mistakes. But the spiritual truth God wanted to convey, most Christians insist, has survived.

Is the Bible more inspired than other Christian literature or sermons?

Some Christians would argue that it is not, on the basis that the Holy Spirit inspired other communicators – as the Bible says the Spirit can do: 'It is not you who will be speaking, but the Holy Spirit' (Mark 13:11).

But most Christians would quickly add that the Bible is the ultimate reliable source of spiritual truth – so reliable that all other spiritual truth must measure up to the teachings in this sacred book. Any teaching out of sync with the Bible would be considered out of sync with God's will.

One thing is clear however: the Bible has passed the test of time. For thousands of years people have studied its message, lived by it, and died for it. It has earned a unique place of honour in humanity's library.

The list of signs could go on, but it would never prove the Bible is God's Word. Yet for countless people throughout the past 3,000 years, it has been enough. They believed.

When sceptical Jewish scholars asked Jesus when he would tell them if he was the promised messiah, he replied, 'I have already told you, and you don't believe me. The proof is what I do in the name of my Father' (John 10:25).

The Bible is much the same. Its writers claim to deliver God's message, and the proof is in what they say in the name of the Father. It's our decision whether or not to believe.

God still speaks

Is the Bible God's only word for us today?

Most Christians believe the Bible contains everything we need to know about him, and about how to live the kind of life he wants us to live.

But there's widespread belief that he still speaks to people, just as he did in ancient times: through the quiet, inner voice of the Holy Spirit as well as through prophecy, dreams, and visions (Acts 2:17). However, most Christians also believe that the Bible is the most effective way to measure the authenticity of any such message. If the message runs contrary to Bible teaching, it's considered to be fake.

Who's who in the Bible

There are more than 3,000 human beings in the Bible. Here are ten of the most important Bible characters.

1. *Noah, a man whose family was spared in the flood (before 2500 BC).* God told Noah and his sons to build a huge boat, to save themselves and land animals from the flood he was going to send to cleanse the earth of sin. 'Noah was a righteous man, the only blameless man living on earth at the time' (Genesis 6:9).

2. *Abraham, father of the Jewish people (2100s BC).* At God's command, he left what is now Iraq and moved to what is now Israel. Once Abraham arrived there, God made him a promise: 'Look as far as you can see in every direction. I am going to give all this land to you and your offspring as a permanent possession. And I am going to give you so many descendants that, like dust, they cannot be counted!' (Genesis 13:14–16).

Noah's ark was designed like a floating warehouse, about 135 meters long, 22 meters wide and 13 meters high (450, 75 and 45 feet).

3. *Jacob, father of Israel's twelve tribes (1900s BC).* Son of Isaac and grandson of Abraham, Jacob produced a dozen sons whose descendants grew to become the twelve tribes of Israel. Each tribe took its ancestor's name. The nation took the name God gave to Jacob: 'Your name will no longer be Jacob… It is now Israel' (Genesis 32:28).

4. *Moses, the leader who freed the Israelites from Egyptian slavery, organized them into a nation, and led them home (1400s or 1200s BC).* God gave Moses the Ten Commandments and the hundreds of other laws based on it – laws that dealt with spiritual, civil, and criminal matters.

5. *David, Israel's most revered king (1000 BC).* Second king of Israel, after Saul. He secured the nation's borders and established Jerusalem as his political capital. Then he brought to Jerusalem the Israelite's most sacred object – the chest that held the Ten Commandments (the Ark of the Covenant). This established Jerusalem as Israel's spiritual center. David was also a musician, and many songs in Psalms are attributed to him.

6. *Solomon, David's son and successor, and builder of Israel's first temple (900s BC).* The Bible describes him as the richest king of his time, with wisdom 'such as no one else has ever had or ever will have!' (1 Kings 3:12). He married 1,000 women, and he wrote 1,005 songs and 3,000 proverbs. Many sayings in the book of Proverbs are attributed to him. Tragically, in old age he worshipped the false gods that his wives followed.

7. *Isaiah, a prophet in Jerusalem who wrote so many prophecies about Jesus that many experts call his book the Fifth Gospel (700s BC).* His most famous prophecy is one that New Testament writers said points to the suffering of Jesus: 'who among the people realized that he was dying for their sins' (Isaiah 53:8). Jewish tradition said Isaiah was cut in two by a wooden saw, at the order of King Manasseh – a notoriously evil Israelite king.

8. *Mary, mother of Jesus (first Christian century).* A young virgin engaged to a carpenter named Joseph, she conceived her divine child by the Holy Spirit. After the birth story, New Testament writers rarely mentioned her.

9. *Peter, leader of Jesus' disciples (first Christian century).* He's most famous for trying to protect himself during Jesus' trial by denying he was a disciple of Jesus. Several weeks later,

The Trinity

The word *Trinity* is not found in the Bible. Church leaders coined the term in the third century AD to describe the divine trio at work throughout history.

God the Father, Creator and sustainer of everything that exists. Holy and perfect in love and justice. All-powerful and eternal. Patiently working to save humanity from the harmful effects of sin.

God the Son, Jesus Christ. Present with God at Creation, and sent by God to earth in human form to die for the sins of humanity. Raised to life again by God, he became the source of a pivotal Christian belief: all who trust in Jesus will be saved from their sins and will live forever with him.

God the Spirit, the agent of Creation, and sent in Old Testament times to empower special leaders such as prophets and select kings. After the return of Jesus to heaven, God sent the Holy Spirit to guide all Christians in their spiritual journey.

Only once does the Bible refer to all three persons of the Trinity in a single verse. Just before his ascension, Jesus told his followers, 'Go and make disciples of all the nations, baptizing them in the name of the Father and the Son and the Holy Spirit' (Matthew 28:19).

For centuries, church leaders debated the nature of the three divine entities. Some said Jesus was simply God on earth and that the Holy Spirit was another name for God. Jesus did say 'The Father and I are one' (John 10:30), but he prayed to his Father, too.

In time, church leaders gave up trying to explain how three could be one. They simply believed it because the Bible taught it. Augustine, a theologian in the AD 400s, summed up the consensus: 'The Father is God, the Son is God, the Holy Spirit is God... yet we do not say that there are three gods, but one God, the most exalted Trinity.'

however, he preached a bold sermon in that same city – converting 3,000 people to a movement that became Christianity. Church leaders at least as early as the AD 200s said that the Romans crucified him upside down in Rome about 35 years after Jesus died.

10. *Paul, author of nearly half the New Testament books, travelled some 10,000 miles starting churches throughout the Roman Empire (first Christian century).* Most of his work was among non-Jews. More than any early church leader, he distanced Christianity from Judaism by insisting that Christians didn't need to observe Jewish customs, such as circumcision and kosher food restrictions.

Where's where in the Bible

Stories in the Bible take place throughout the Middle East –
from what is now Iran on the eastern edge to Italy and Egypt
on the western side. Here are ten of the most famous Bible
locations.

1. *Babylon, the name of both a capital city and an empire that
dominated the ancient Middle East and wiped the Jewish nation off
the world map in 586 BC.* The empire's capital was near what
is now Baghdad. Many years later, the Persians conquered
Babylon and allowed the Jews to rebuild their nation. In the
first Christian century, Babylon became a code name for Rome,
because both empires destroyed Jerusalem.

2. *Bethlehem, home town of King David and birthplace of Jesus.*
'But you, O Bethlehem Ephrathah, are only a small village in
Judah. Yet a ruler of Israel will come from you, one whose
origins are from the distant past... he will be the source of
our peace' (Micah 5:2, 5). New Testament writers read this
as a prophecy about Jesus.

3. *Capernaum, home town of Peter and the ministry headquarters of
Jesus.* Nearly half of Jesus' twelve disciples lived in this fishing
village by the Sea of Galilee. It was here that Jesus healed
many people and taught new ideas that enraged Jewish
scholars.

4. *Egypt, the Nile River nation famous for the exodus Moses led.*
Jacob and his extended family fled to Egypt to escape a
famine, but their descendants were eventually enslaved
there. Moses led them to freedom. Throughout Bible
times, Egypt jockeyed for position as a world superpower,
sometimes allying itself with Israel and sometimes attacking
them.

5. *Israel, the land God promised to Abraham's descendants 'as a
permanent possession'* (Genesis 13:15). This Jewish homeland
was twice erased from the world map, first for fifty years in
the 500s BC, when Babylon invaded, and then for 1,900 years

when Rome crushed a rebellion in AD 70. The modern nation of Israel was formed in 1948.

6. *Jerusalem, capital and religious center for the people of Israel.* King David conquered what was a tiny, ridge-top city in southern Israel and turned it into his capital. His son, Solomon, built the first of three Jewish temples there on a hilltop now occupied by the 1,300-year-old Dome of the Rock – a Muslim shrine.

7. *Judah, name of the southern nation of Israel after it split in two.* The northern nation took the name Israel. The southern nation's name came from the largest tribe in the south, Judah.

8. *Mount Sinai, where God gave Moses the Ten Commandments and many other laws preserved in the Old Testament.* Several months earlier, God appeared to Moses in a burning bush near this mountain and told him to free the Israelites in Egypt.

9. *Sea of Galilee, a freshwater lake whose shores became the stage for most of Jesus' miracles and teachings.* Several of Jesus' disciples were fishing there when he invited them to follow

Fishermen cruise along the shoreline of the Sea of Galilee, a freshwater lake where several of Jesus' disciples had worked on fishing crews.

him. Jesus walked on the waters of this lake, and he used the lakeside village of Capernaum as his headquarters.

10. *Nazareth, the hilltop village in northern Israel where Jesus grew up as a carpenter's son.* When he later returned home as a famous prophet, the villagers rejected him and tried to 'push him over the cliff, but he slipped away through the crowd and left them' (Luke 4:29–30).

How to read the Bible

Don't think of the Bible as a book.

Think of it as a library of 66 books, written by a huge gallery of writers, each with a different reason for writing and each living in a different situation – in settings that stretch across more than a millennium. Every one of these books needs to be read on its own terms.

We don't read history the way we read an emotionally charged letter. And we don't read the stylized writings of a poet the way we read the precise prose of a lawyer. If a lawyer says the punishment for adultery is death, we'd probably take that literally. But if a poet said that, we'd wonder if adultery and death are symbols for something else. It's a fact that sometimes in the Bible 'adultery' refers to Israel's sin of abandoning God for idols. And 'death' can refer to what happened to Israel after God sent invaders to punish the nation.

To get to the meaning of a particular statement in the Bible, it is worth asking several questions.

What kind of writing is it?

In the Bible there are laws, history, poetry, song lyrics, wise sayings, prophecies, eye-witness reports about Jesus, and letters.

One style of writing that is often misread is apocalyptic prophecy, which we find in some of the writings of Daniel, Ezekiel and Zechariah, and throughout Revelation. These are warnings about coming disaster, which often seem to refer to the end of human history. Many readers take these prophetic words literally. But the writing style that was used in times of oppression featured coded language and symbols to make it difficult for the oppressors – the Romans in the time Revelation was written – to understand what the writers were talking about.

In recent years, during troubled times in the Middle East,

there has been a temptation to speculate that the word 'Babylon' in Revelation is a literal reference to Iraq, because Babylon's ruins lie on the outskirts of Baghdad. But among Jews in New Testament times, 'Babylon' was a code word for 'Rome.' That's because the Romans – like the Babylonians 600 years earlier – destroyed Jerusalem and its temple.

The poetry of Psalms – as well as poems woven into prophecy – is also misread frequently, with readers taking the words more literally than the psalmists intended.

Roman soldiers carry treasure looted from the Jewish temple they destroyed. This scene chiseled in stone commemorates Rome crushing a Jewish rebellion in AD 70. The Jerusalem temple was never rebuilt.

Who wrote it and why?

To many Bible readers, 1 and 2 Chronicles read like a sugar-coated version of stories in 1–2 Samuel and 1–2 Kings that leave out the bad parts of Israel's history – such as King David's adultery with Bathsheba and the murder of her husband.

But Chronicles was written much later. The Jews knew the sad story of their past all too well, but the writer of Chronicles was trying to isolate carefully selected scenes from their history to encourage them about their future. The Jews had just returned from exile to a demolished nation. They had broken their covenant with God by disobeying him, and they had suffered the consequences. Standing in the ashes of Jerusalem, they worried that they were no longer God's chosen people. The writer used an upbeat version of their nation's story to assure them that God had always been with them – and still was. They were still the chosen.

In the New Testament, the four Gospels overlap quite a bit in their stories about Jesus. But each writer has his own slant, which emphasizes different points. Matthew wants to show that Jesus fulfils Old Testament prophecies about the messiah, so he quotes almost 60 prophecies. John wants to convince readers that Jesus is God, so he homes in on teachings and miracles that help to prove his divinity.

What was going on at the time?

Unless we know how much the Jews and Samaritans hated each other, we don't get the full kick in the face that Jesus' parable of the Good Samaritan delivered to Jewish leaders.

Jews considered Samaritans to be half breeds by race and religion. When Assyrians overran the northern land of Samaria in the 700s BC and occupied it with their own pioneers, many of the Jews who survived eventually married these settlers and apparently incorporated some aspects of the foreign religion into the Jewish faith.

Seven hundred years of animosity between the Jews and Samaritans – who shared what is now Israel – gradually escalated until it rivalled the hatred and distrust that exists between Palestinians and Israelis in modern times. Jews travelling between Jerusalem and Galilee usually took a long detour around Samaria – a region directly between the two communities.

In Jesus' parable, intended to teach us who exactly is our

In search of a verse

Most books about the Bible – this one included – use a common code to point readers to particular Bible passages. If you're directed to John 3:16, for example:

John = book of the Bible

3 = chapter

16 = verse

neighbour in the command 'love your neighbour', a Jewish man was robbed and beaten nearly to death while walking on the isolated trail between Jerusalem and Jericho. A Jewish priest walked by, ignoring the victim. A temple worker did the same. It was a Samaritan who helped the Jewish man and who paid for his care.

A neighbour, Jesus graphically revealed, is anyone who needs our help. Anyone. There's no room for prejudice among citizens of God's kingdom.

Tips for getting the most from the Bible

● **Read it regularly.** Whether we're a morning person or a night person, we can set up a daily routine for reading the Bible. We can start our day with some reading, use it as a midday break, or bring our day to a close with its words.

● **Choose a manageable amount to read.** Some people have time to read several chapters a day. Others only have time for a few verses. Whether we're reading printed Bibles or digital ones, we can tailor the amount of our reading to fit our schedule. The key point to remember is that if we don't read at least something from the Bible, it can't do us any good.

● **Pick a readable translation.** The *King James Version* was written in Shakespeare's time and is hard for most people to understand – though many believe the beauty of its writing is still unsurpassed by modern versions. Yet the beauty of the cadence and the lyrical flow doesn't mean much if we can't figure out the message. It's the message, not the writing style, that's most important. We should pick a version that speaks our language.

One hundred hours long

Reading aloud at a typical pace, a person can finish the Bible in less than 100 hours.

● **Don't read it from cover to cover, like a novel.** Many people who start at the beginning

Favourite Bible study tools

- **Study Bible.** These Bibles have notes in the margins, which answer questions about the passages and add insights and historical background. Some study Bibles have nearly as many notes as they do Bible text.

- **Bible guide book.** Books like the one you're reading introduce the Bible to new readers and provide clues about how to get more out of studying it.

- **One-volume commentary.** With more detailed notes than a study Bible, one-volume Bible commentaries offer insights on every book of the Bible. There are also single-volume commentaries on individual books of the Bible for even more in-depth study.

- **Atlas.** A good Bible atlas provides a collection of maps that illustrate important Bible stories, such as Abraham's move to what is now Israel and Moses leading the Israelites out of Egypt. Some atlases even plot troop movements in battles such as Joshua's conquest of the Promised Land.

- **Bible dictionary or encyclopedia.** These provide short articles about people, places, customs, teachings and objects – just about any kind of Bible background topic you can imagine. Many of these books are heavily illustrated, which improves understanding all the more.

- **Bible study software.** These software packages are digital libraries containing all the above and usually much more. The cost of a digital library is far less than the cost of the same material in printed forms. They generally include many different translations of the Bible, multiple commentaries and a collection of devotional books.

of the Bible run out of steam once they hit the strange Jewish laws and long genealogies. We should read the Bible like a library. Pick a book that interests us. Perhaps a story about Jesus – the Gospel of Mark is the shortest and most lively. Or maybe a letter about how to live the Christian life – something like Ephesians or Philippians. One extra tip: resist the temptation to read the end-times book of Revelation first; the best biblical experts are still trying to figure out that book!

- **React to what you read.** Think about the words. The truth of the Bible can adjust our attitudes and brighten our lives. That's in the Bible's job description, as Paul explained in a letter to his friend: 'All Scripture is inspired by God and is useful to teach us what is true and to make us realize what is wrong in our lives. It straightens us out and teaches us to do what is right' (2 Timothy 3:16).

Popular ways to study the Bible

Though there are many ways to study the Bible, the most common are:

● **Book by book.** Select a book of the Bible, and read it through – perhaps a chapter or just a few verses at a time. When something we read sparks a question, we can look for answers in Bible study resources – such as notes in the margin of a study Bible or in commentaries.

● **By topic.** Select an intriguing topic, such as prayer, divorce or heaven. Then look for all the Bible passages that deal with the topic. A topical concordance lists different topics alphabetically, alongside related Bible passages.

Here's a caution when using the topical approach: consider the context of each passage. Some material may refer to a specific situation in ancient times, while others may be presented as general truths for all to live by.

The Bible Jesus read

A quick peek

The Bible Jesus read, which Christians call the Old Testament, is about twice as long as the New Testament. That makes it two-thirds of the Holy Bible.

It probably took more than 1,000 years for Jews to compile the 39 books of the Old Testament – from around the time of King David to Jesus. In fact, by the time Jesus began his ministry around AD 30, the Jewish scriptures in their final form may have been just a couple of hundred years old – or less.

The Old Testament preserves ancient stories of God at work in the world long before the Jewish race developed, and long after the Jewish nation faded into the shadows of powerful empires such as the Assyrians, Babylonians, Persians, Greeks and Romans.

Highlights from the Bible that Jesus studied as a child include:

● God creates everything that exists.

● Humans choose to disobey God, alienating themselves from him.

● God sends a flood, killing everyone but the family of righteous Noah – a fresh start for humanity.

● God selects Abraham to become father of the Jews – a nation chosen to show the world what righteousness looks like.

● The Israelites fail God, breaking even his most basic laws.

● God sends invaders to erase Israel from the world map, scattering the survivors abroad.

● God brings the Jewish remnant home, forgiven – another fresh start.

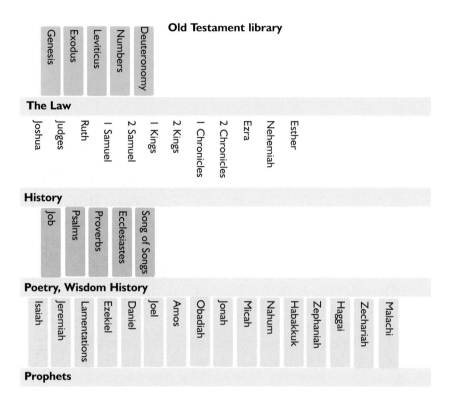

Old Testament library

The Law: Genesis, Exodus, Leviticus, Numbers, Deuteronomy

History: Joshua, Judges, Ruth, 1 Samuel, 2 Samuel, 1 Kings, 2 Kings, 1 Chronicles, 2 Chronicles, Ezra, Nehemiah, Esther

Poetry, Wisdom History: Job, Psalms, Proverbs, Ecclesiastes, Song of Songs

Prophets: Isiah, Jeremiah, Lamentations, Ezekiel, Daniel, Joel, Amos, Obadiah, Jonah, Micah, Nahum, Habakkuk, Zephaniah, Haggai, Zechariah, Malachi

By the book

Genesis

● *In a paragraph:*

God creates a perfect world and a human couple to rule it. They break God's only law, eating forbidden fruit. This sin destroys their intimate relationship with God, and somehow damages the creation. Ten generations later, sin is so pervasive that God starts again by flooding the world and killing everyone but Noah and his family. God later calls a righteous man named Abraham to move to what is now Israel and become the father of the Israelites, a people devoted to him. Abraham's grandson, Jacob, moves the extended family to Egypt during a drought. In time, they will become a race of slaves who will need God to free them, through Moses.

What good is this ancient history today?

Two thousand years old is as modern as the Bible gets. That's when Jesus lived and that's about how long ago writers penned the final books in this ancient collection. And some material is more than a thousand years older than that, dating back to the time of Moses.

How can these writings still be relevant? We all know that today, one generation tends to reject as obsolete the experiences and advice of the previous generation. And with the Bible, we're talking about 100 generations ago – and that's for the most recent material.

Yet this book of the ancients has remained a best-seller throughout the ages, ever since a German printer named Johann Gutenberg began publishing it in the 1450s, as the first project for his newly invented printing press.

● **Bible principles still apply.** The Bible contains a lot of ideas that just don't fit today's culture. The social welfare system, for example, took care of widows who had no sons; but it did so by requiring the dead husband's brother to marry the woman. Because of this, women – who by custom couldn't own property – were saved from poverty and prostitution. This system may no longer be relevant, but the principle of helping the helpless is just as important as it ever was. The most vulnerable people in Bible times were widows, orphans and immigrants. It's up to us to determine who are the most vulnerable today, and then to help them.

● **The main teachings are timeless.** The message of the Bible revolves around the Ten Commandments, most of which remain the foundation for legal codes in countries throughout the world today. And the Ten Commandments summed up in one sentence become the Golden Rule: treat others the way you want to be treated. Those of us who have been on the planet for a few decades know the value of that teaching. When we give a smile, we're likely to get a smile in return. Give a growl, and we can expect a growl back.

● **We learn from the mistakes and successes of others.** The Bible is full of case studies – often of people learning their lessons the hard way: lessons about what happens when we commit adultery, play favourites in the family, or chase money by exploiting the helpless. When we read these case studies, we can learn from them. It's a bit like going to college. Instead of learning from the experience of a generation of professors, we're learning from the experience of countless generations. And these are lessons validated by Christians over 2,000 years – lessons that have stood the test of time and are still revered throughout the world.

Replica of Johann Gutenberg's workshop and printing press that produced history's first printed Bible.

● *Key point:*
God is the source and sustainer of creation, and he calls a people to be devoted to him.

● *Author, date:*
Unknown. Jewish tradition says Moses, in 1400s or 1200s BC.

● *Main characters:*
Adam and Eve, the first humans
Noah, who survives the flood
Abraham, his son Isaac, and his grandson Jacob, fathers of the Israelites
Joseph, one of Jacob's sons, sold as a slave to Egypt

● *Biggest scene:*
Over six days, which many experts say should not be taken as twenty-four-hour days, God creates everything that exists in the universe. On the seventh day, he rests – a practice the Jews later observe as the Sabbath (Genesis 1:1–2:2).

● *Most famous line:*
'In the beginning God created the heavens and the earth' (Genesis 1:1).

Exodus

● *In a paragraph:*
Jacob's extended family of 70 people, who had migrated to Egypt to escape a drought in Israel, grows to thousands. The Egyptian king fears they will overrun the nation, so he enslaves them. After 430 years in Egypt – the Bible doesn't say how much of that was in slavery – they are led to freedom by Moses. But it takes ten plagues to convince the king to release them. And afterwards, the king changes his mind and leads

Creation in six days?

God made the universe in six days, the Bible says. But were they twenty-four-hour days? Not necessarily, argue many Bible experts. Twenty-four-hour days didn't exist until day four, when God created the sun and moon 'to mark off the seasons, the days and the years' (Genesis 1:14). Six days may have simply referred to an unknown stretch of time – perhaps seconds, days or aeons.

his chariot unit to bring them back. His army is drowned when they follow the fugitives into an escape path God made for the Israelites – a path through the sea. The Israelites camp for around a year at Mount Sinai, where Moses receives the Ten Commandments and hundreds of other laws that organize the people into a nation.

● *Key point:*
God steps into human history and miraculously frees the Israelites from slavery in Egypt and establishes them as an independent nation with a unique set of laws.

Ramses II, perhaps the Egyptian king Moses dealt with, joins his wife Queen Nefertari in worshipping Hathor, goddess of the sky.

Ten commandments

The Ten Commandments are ten concise laws on which all other Jewish laws rest. Before Moses delivered these ten laws on stone, God spoke them from Mount Sinai – to terrified Israelites assembled on the plain below (Exodus 19–20).

1. Worship only God.

2. Do not make or worship idols.

3. Do not treat God's name disrespectfully.

4. Rest for one day a week.

5. Respect your parents.

6. Do not murder.

7. Do not commit adultery.

8. Do not steal.

9. Do not lie.

10. Do not envy others and crave what they have.

● *Author, date:*
Unknown. Jewish tradition says Moses, in 1400s or 1200s BC.

● *Main characters:*
Moses, leads the Israelites out of Egypt
Aaron, older brother of Moses, and his assistant
Pharaoh, king of Egypt

● *Biggest scene:*
Trapped between a huge body of water and an attacking chariot unit, the fugitive Israelites escape in what becomes one of the most famous miracles of the Bible. God sends an all-night wind that dries a path through the sea (Exodus 14).

● *Most famous line:*
'Let my people go' (Exodus 5:1).

Leviticus

● *In a paragraph:*
Camped for around a year at Mount Sinai, the Israelites organize themselves into a nation.

By the billions, locusts descend on Egypt in 2004 – just as the Bible says they did at the time of Moses, when ten plagues convinced Pharaoh to free the Israelite slaves.

Were the ten plagues natural disasters?

Some Bible experts say the ten plagues that convinced Egypt's king to free the Israelites could have been a string of natural disasters, each one triggering the next.

1. Nile River turns red. Flooding in upstream swamplands releases a type of Red Tide toxic algae. An Egyptian story from Moses' era reported an event similar to the one in the Bible: 'The river is blood. People refuse to drink it.'

2. Frog infestation. Frogs may have fled the polluted river and then died.

3. Insects. Possibly mosquitoes or gnats, bred in pools of water left by the flood.

4. Flies. From eggs laid in decaying objects: wet grain, dead frogs.

5. Sick livestock. Perhaps anthrax, carried by insects.

6. Boils. Anthrax and some insect bites produce blisters and boils.

7. Hail. A common occurrence.

8. Locusts. Also common.

9. Darkness for three days. Possibly sandstorms driven by Khamsin winds from the Sahara Desert.

10. Death of firstborn. Favoured, oldest children sometimes got more food – perhaps food contaminated by mould and disease.

Many other experts, however, insist that looking for natural explanations misses the point. And the point is not how the Israelites were freed, but who freed them. It was God who freed them – however he chose to do it.

Through Moses, God delivers around 600 laws intended to mark out the Israelites as a nation uniquely devoted to God. Some laws are religious, explaining how to worship God with sacrifices. Others deal with civil and criminal problems. The people build a portable worship centre – a tent called the Tabernacle. Aaron becomes the nation's first high priest in charge of worship.

A tent worship centre allowed Moses and the Israelites to worship God wherever they went during the exodus. It wasn't until perhaps three centuries later that the Jews built the Jerusalem temple.

● *Key point:*
God is holy, and his people must be holy — which means completely devoted to him. The laws and rituals he gives them are intended for that purpose: to establish them as a people separated from sin and dedicated to him.

● *Author, date:*
Unknown. Jewish tradition says Moses, in 1400s or 1200s BC.

● *Main characters:*
Moses, leader of the Israelite refugees
Aaron, Moses' brother, who becomes high priest

The Sinai Peninsula — where Moses and the Israelites camped for about a year — is a barren expanse. Water and vegetation are in short supply.

● *Biggest scene:*
Aaron and his sons are ordained as Israel's first priests. They will lead the nation's worship rituals, which are built on a new system of animal sacrifices (Leviticus 8).

● *Most famous line:*
'You must become holy because I am holy' (Leviticus 11:44).

Numbers

● *In a paragraph:*
Moses and the Israelites break their year-long camp at Mount Sinai and head north for what is now Israel – the homeland God had promised them. In spite of God's many miracles, they are quick to complain. And when they reach Canaan's border and hear of giants and walled cities ahead, they refuse to invade. So God orders them to stay out for 40 years. He will wait to lead a new and braver generation into the land.

● *Key point:*
God punishes sin – a fact he illustrates many times, but most dramatically by sentencing the Israelites to 40 years in the Judean badlands for refusing to invade the Promised Land.

Why blood sacrifices?

Animals have been dying because of humanity's sin almost from the beginning of time – since Adam and Eve sinned in the Garden of Eden and God made animal-skin clothing to hide their nakedness.

But why did God later tell the Israelites to seek forgiveness by sacrificing animals?

'The life of any creature is in its blood. I have given you the blood so you can make atonement for your sins. It is the blood, representing life, that brings you atonement' (Leviticus 17:11).

Sin is serious – a capital offence in God's eyes. The sin of Adam and Eve brought death into the world. Animal sacrifices not only served as graphic reminders of how serious sin is – they served as substitutes for the sinners.

Jesus' crucifixion rendered that sacrificial system obsolete. No longer did people have to sacrifice animals whenever they sinned, because Jesus' death in their place made them right with God for ever.

'Jesus did this once for all when he sacrificed himself on the cross.' (Hebrews 7:27)

● *Author, date:*
Unknown. Jewish tradition says Moses, in 1400s or 1200s BC.

● *Main characters:*
Moses, leader of the Israelite refugees
Aaron, Moses' brother and Israel's high priest
Joshua, warrior and scout

● *Biggest scene:*
A dozen scouts, including Joshua, return to camp with a mixed report about the Promised Land, now called Israel. It's fertile, but has large, fortified cities – and a race of giants among the many inhabitants. Terrified, the Israelites refuse to invade (Numbers 13–14).

● *Most famous line:*
'The Lord bless you and keep you; The Lord make His face shine upon you, And be gracious to you; The Lord lift up His countenance upon you, And give you peace' (Numbers 6:24–26).

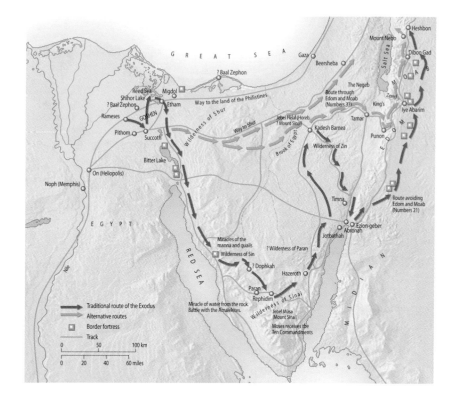

Route of the Exodus, from Egypt to what is now Israel.

Deuteronomy

● **In a paragraph:**
Poised for invasion into the Promised Land from their camp in what is now Jordan, the Israelites say goodbye to the only leader most of them have ever known. Moses is about to die. So he assembles the people and gives them a history lesson: he reminds them of all that God has done for them; and he reviews the laws God has given them, along with the blessings they can expect if they obey – and the punishment if they don't. 'Today I have given you the choice between life and death, between blessings and curses,' he says. 'Oh, that you would choose life' (Deuteronomy 30:19).

● **Key point:**
Faith is a decision. We can choose God, and the blessings that come from serving him; or we can choose sin, and the tragic

Why order a Canaanite extermination?

On the brink of launching an invasion into Canaan – now Israel – Moses gives this advice to the Israelite warriors:
'As for the towns of the nations the Lord your God is giving you as a special possession, destroy every living thing in them.' [This includes all men, women, and children.]
    'This will keep the people of the land from teaching you their detestable customs in the worship of their gods' (Deuteronomy 20: 16, 18).

Worship in Canaan included human sacrifice, especially of babies. Worshippers also had ritual sex with temple prostitutes, to stimulate the gods to make families, flocks, and fields fertile. God intended to cleanse the land of this sin, much as he had done during the flood in Noah's time.
    Unfortunately, Moses' warning comes true. Canaanite survivors eventually teach the Israelites how to worship their gods. Within a few centuries, the Israelites will become so pagan that God will cleanse the land of them, too.

consequences that will follow. The choice is ours. The results are inevitable.

● *Author, date:*
Unknown. Jewish tradition says Moses, in 1400s or 1200s BC.

● *Main characters:*
Moses, Israelite leader who dies
Joshua, successor to Moses

● *Biggest scene:*
Moses, now 120 years old, climbs Mount Nebo in what is now Jordan and looks west across the Jordan River valley into the Promised Land. It's as close as he will ever get to Israel, for he dies on the mountain (Deuteronomy 34).

● *Most famous line:*
'Love the Lord your God with all your heart, all your soul, and all your strength' (Deuteronomy 6:5).

Baal, the chief Canaanite god. This gold-plated figurine was crafted about the time Joshua led the Israelites on their conquest of Canaan, modern-day Israel.

Joshua

● *In a paragraph:*

After spending 430 years in Egypt – much of that as slaves – and then 40 years in the Judean badlands, the Israelites begin their fight for a homeland in Canaan. Moses has died. But God assures Joshua, the new leader, 'Everywhere you go, you will be on land I have given you… No one will be able to stand their ground against you as long as you live' (Joshua 1:3, 5). The Israelites crush fortified towns in the south and then move north. With much of the hilly countryside captured, Joshua divides the land among the twelve tribes and assigns each tribe to mop up their individual regions. The people then make a contract with God to get rid of their foreign gods and serve him only.

● *Key point:*

As long as the Israelites devote themselves to God, they can trust that God will fight their battles for them. Even before the invasion begins, God describes the victory in the past tense: 'Take possession of the land the Lord your God has given you' (Joshua 1:11).

● *Author, date:*

Unknown. The story is set in the 1400s or the 1200s BC.

● *Main character:*

Joshua, the new leader of the Israelites

Jericho was a border town in this large oasis along the Jordan River valley, just below the Judean hills.

● *Biggest scene:*

The walls of Jericho miraculously come tumbling down – the first Canaanite city to fall during the Israelite conquest (Joshua 6).

● *Most famous line:*
'... as for me and my family, we will serve the Lord.' (Joshua 24:15)

Judges

● *In a paragraph:*
Joshua has died, trusting the Israelites to finish off the Canaanites and serve God. They do neither. They adopt Canaanite religion, breaking their contract with God and suffering the consequences listed in the contract. Invaders victimize them. The Israelites call on God for help, and he sends a deliverer called a 'judge'. This cycle of sin, repentance and deliverance happens at least a dozen times, but the book ends with the people living in anarchy: 'The people did whatever seemed right in their own eyes' (Judges 21:25).

● *Key point:*
God is relentlessly loving and merciful. He punishes sin, but when people repent, he forgives them and rescues them.

● *Author, date:*
Unknown. The stories take place during the two to four centuries before David becomes king in around 1000 BC.

● *Main characters:*
Samson, the book's most famous warrior
Delilah, the woman who subdues him
Gideon, a militia leader
Deborah, the only female leader of Israel in Judges

● *Biggest scene:*
Samson kills a thousand Philistines with a donkey's jawbone. He had allowed his Israelite neighbours to turn him over to the Philistines. But once in Philistine custody, he attacks. People rename the attack site, 'Jawbone Hill' (Judges 15:17).

● *Most famous line:*
'The Israelites did what was evil in the Lord's sight' (Judges 6:1).

Ruth

● *In a paragraph:*
A Bethlehem couple and their two sons move to what is now Jordan, to escape a famine. Both sons marry women there, but within ten years the father and sons all die – leaving their widows destitute in a culture where women can't inherit property. The mother, Naomi, tells her daughters-in-law to go home to their fathers, and that she will go back to Bethlehem. Ruth insists on going with Naomi. In Bethlehem, Ruth meets Boaz, a relative of Naomi's dead husband. He agrees to marry her and take care of Naomi, too. The welfare system of the time calls on relatives of the dead husband to marry the widow. Ruth – a non-Jew – becomes the great-grandmother of Israel's most revered king, David.

● *Key point:*
God loves the people most others ignore: the outcasts, the poor and the powerless. Ruth was such a woman – and she produced Israel's greatest dynasty of kings.

● *Author, date:*
Unknown, though Jewish tradition says Samuel wrote it. Ruth probably lived in the 1100s BC.

● *Main characters:*
Ruth, a widow and great-grandmother of King David
Naomi, Ruth's mother-in-law
Boaz, Ruth's second husband and great-grandfather of David

● *Biggest scene:*
Ruth refuses to let her widowed mother-in-law, Naomi, face poverty alone. They both walk from what is now Jordan to Bethlehem, in the hope that someone in Naomi's extended family will take them in (Ruth 1).

● *Most famous line:*
'I will go wherever you go and live wherever you live. Your people will be my people, and your God will be my God' (Ruth 1:16).

1 Samuel

● *In a paragraph:*
Israel isn't satisfied with God as king. They want a human king, like other nations. The prophet Samuel, at God's command, anoints Saul as the first king of Israel. Saul grows insanely jealous of David, who soars in popularity after killing the Philistine champion, Goliath. Saul disobeys God by offering a sacrifice before a battle – a ritual that only a priest can perform. So God rejects him and orders Samuel to secretly anoint David as the future king. Saul and three of his sons die in a battle that Israel loses to the Philistines.

● *Key point:*
'People judge by outward appearance, but the Lord looks at a person's thoughts and intentions' (1 Samuel 16:7).

● *Author, date:*
Unknown. The stories take place during the 1000s BC.

● *Main characters:*
Samuel, a prophet
Saul, Israel's first king
David, the giant-killer who will become Israel's most famous king

● *Biggest scene:*
Armed with a slingshot, shepherd boy David kills the Philistine champion, a giant named Goliath. Though Goliath is bristling with the best

Goliath

Massive height along with state-of-the-art weaponry gives the Philistine champion, Goliath, a big advantage over David – a shepherd boy armed with a slingshot.

Height: over 2 metres (nearly 7 feet). Some texts say 3 metres (nearly 10 feet).

Coat of mail: 57 kilograms (125 pounds).

Metal weapons: crafted from newly-discovered iron, which can slice through Israel's bronze weapons.

Spear shaft: the size of a 'weaver's beam,' about 5 centimetres thick (2 inches), or more.

Spearhead: 6.8 kilograms (15 pounds).

Armour bearer: an assistant carrying a shield.

Shepherd boy near Bethlehem, where David grew up.

weaponry of the day, a tiny stone stops him (1 Samuel 17:49).

● *Most famous line:*
'Obedience is far better than sacrifice' (1 Samuel 15:22).

2 Samuel

● *In a paragraph:*
With Saul dead, Israel rallies around heroic David, the giant-killer, crowning him king. A masterful warrior, David overpowers the Philistines, secures Israel's borders and dominates the Middle East deep into what is now Jordan and Syria. Widely respected as a national leader, he proves himself a feeble husband and father. He has an affair, gets the woman pregnant, and then orders her husband killed so he can marry her. And he doesn't discipline one of his sons, who rapes a half-sister. That prods the victim's full brother to murder the rapist and to launch a coup against David.

● *Key point:*
There is no sin too big for God's mercy. God forgives a repentant David even for adultery and murder.

● *Author, date:*
Unknown. The stories take place during the 1000s BC.

● *Main characters:*
David, Israel's second king
Nathan, a prophet and David's adviser
Absalom, David's son who dies leading a coup

● *Biggest scene:*
The very married King David – who has at least seven wives – takes an afternoon walk on his roof. He sees Bathsheba, the wife of a soldier, taking a bath below, probably in her walled courtyard. David sends for her to come to the palace and has sexual relations with her. She becomes pregnant (2 Samuel 11).

● *Most famous line:*
'How the mighty have fallen!' (2 Samuel 1:19).

1 Kings

● *In a paragraph:*
David dies and transfers leadership to his son, Solomon, who leads the nation during its most prosperous generation. In this golden era, Solomon builds the Jerusalem temple, the palace and fortified cities throughout the country. But his politically-linked marriages to a thousand women eventually lure him into idolatry. After Solomon dies, his son threatens to tax the people more than ever. The nation splits into north and south, leaving Solomon's son to rule only the southern nation of Judah. God calls on prophets such as Elijah to speak out against evil rulers in both nations, including King Ahab and Queen Jezebel in the north.

● *Key point:*
God rewards obedience and punishes sin. Solomon's family loses half of the kingdom because Solomon 'turned away from the Lord' (1 Kings 11:9).

● *Author, date:*
Unknown. This history of Israel spans around a century, starting with Solomon's reign in around 970 BC.

● *Main characters:*
Solomon, David's son and the next king
Elijah, a prophet
Ahab and Jezebel, king and queen of what becomes the northern Israelite nation

● *Biggest scene:*
While deciding a court case, Solomon offers to cut a baby

A reconstruction of Israel's first temple. King Solomon ordered the temple built in Jerusalem, where it stood for nearly 400 years before Babylonian invaders tore it down.

47

boy in two. He says he'll give one piece to each of the two prostitutes who claim they are the boy's mother. One woman agrees, but the other says, 'Give her the child – please do not kill him!' (1 Kings 3:26). The true mother wins back her son. Solomon wins a reputation for wisdom.

● *Most famous line:*
'God gave Solomon great wisdom and understanding, and knowledge too vast to be measured.' (1 Kings 4:29)

2 Kings

● *In a paragraph:*
God's ancient contract with the Israelite people says that if they persist in disobeying him, he will take away their homeland and scatter them 'among all the nations from one end of the earth to the other' (Deuteronomy 28:64). They persist. God sends several generations of prophets to warn them, but they rarely manage to affect the people. First the northern Israelite nation falls, invaded by Assyria. Around 150 years later, Babylon erases the last Israelite nation from the map, exiling survivors to what is now Iraq. Israel becomes nothing but a memory.

● *Key point:*
Though God is patient and merciful, he doesn't ignore sin. In time, he allows the tragic consequences to take their course. Sin causes death.

● *Author, date:*
Unknown. This part of the history of Israel stretches from around 850 BC, until the last Israelite nation is wiped off the world map in 586 BC.

This clay prism contains Assyrian King Sennacherib's report that he destroyed 46 Israelite cities. It doesn't, however, claim that the army captured Jerusalem. Substantiating the Bible's account that Sennacherib's army managed only to surround Jerusalem, the report quotes the king saying: 'I made [Hezekiah] a prisoner in Jerusalem, his royal residence, like a bird in a cage.'

● *Main characters:*
Elijah and Elisha, partnered prophets
Jezebel, queen of Israel
Hezekiah, a godly king of Judah

● *Biggest scene:*
After a lifetime of ministry, the prophet Elijah is swept up into the heavens by a whirlwind and a chariot of fire (2 Kings 2:11).

● *Most famous line:*
'He did what was evil in the Lord's sight' (2 Kings 3:2).

Jehu on the record

Israel's King Jehu – the former warrior who led the coup that ended Ahab and Jezebel's family dynasty – once bowed to an Assyrian king. A stone inscription recovered from the Assyrian capital says 'Jehu, son of Omri' brought gifts of gold and silver.

---

1 Chronicles

● *In a paragraph:*
After tracing the Israelite family tree back to Adam, the writer retells stories from the time of Israel's first two kings, Saul and David. For many readers, the two books of Chronicles read like a political spin doctor's version of stories in 1, 2 Samuel and 1, 2 Kings – only without the scandals. There's no word of Saul's jealously towards David; nothing of David's affair with Bathsheba. But the writer wasn't sugar-coating history. He wrote for Jews who had returned to a decimated Israel, wondering if they were still God's chosen people and if this was still their Promised Land. Focusing on upbeat stories of God at work among the Israelites in earlier times, the writer answers 'yes' to both questions.

● *Key point:*
God never gives up on people. Even after wiping Israel off the world map because of their centuries of sin, he brings them home and gives them a fresh start.

● *Author, date:*
Unknown, though Jewish tradition says the priest Ezra wrote it in the 400s BC. The stories take place when Kings Saul and David ruled Israel in the 1000s BC.

David leads a procession bringing the Ark of the Covenant to Jerusalem.

● *Main characters:*
Saul, Israel's first king
David, Israel's most famous king

● *Biggest scene:*
'Dancing and leaping for joy,' King David brings Israel's most sacred object to Jerusalem: the Ark of the Covenant, a gold-covered chest containing the Ten Commandments (1 Chronicles 15). Jerusalem becomes Israel's political and spiritual capital.

● *Most famous line:*
'Give thanks to the Lord, for he is good! His faithful love endures forever' (1 Chronicles 16:34).

2 Chronicles

● *In a paragraph:*
Written to encourage Jews returning from exile to rebuild

Israel, this book traces the history of Israel's kings – focusing mainly on the godly ones. Solomon leads the nation through its most glorious era. Hezekiah saves his people from an invasion. Yet the writer says that in time – because of the people's sin – the Israelite nation falls to Babylon and the survivors are exiled. Afterwards, the Persian King Cyrus lets the exiled Jews go home – an act of God's mercy that had been predicted by the prophets of Israel.

● *Key point:*
Individuals and nations devoted to God enjoy his blessing and care. And for remorseful sinners, there is forgiveness and restoration.

● *Author, date:*
Unknown, though Jewish tradition says the priest Ezra wrote it in the 400s BC. The book starts with the reign of King Solomon in around 970 BC, continues through the destruction of Judah in 586 BC, and ends with Jewish exiles coming home to rebuild their nation 50 years later.

● *Main characters:*
Solomon, the king of Israel during their most prosperous generation
Hezekiah, a godly king who saves the southern nation of Judah from Assyrian invaders

● *Biggest scene:*
When Solomon builds the first Jewish temple, a jewel of architecture and beauty set into a Jerusalem hilltop, God arrives. 'A cloud filled the Temple of the Lord. The priests could not continue their work because the glorious presence of the Lord filled the Temple of God' (2 Chronicles 5:13–14).

● *Most famous line:*
'If my people who are called by my name will humble themselves and pray and seek my face and turn from their wicked ways, I will hear from heaven and will forgive their sins and heal their land' (2 Chronicles 7:14).

Ezra

● *In a paragraph:*
After living for 50 years in exile in Babylon – modern-day Iraq – the Jews are free to go home and rebuild their nation. Persia has defeated the conqueror of the Jews, Babylon, and has freed all captives. Some Jews stay behind, but many return to Jerusalem and rebuild their temple. A priest named Ezra arrives around a century later, in the mid-400s BC, and takes a leading role in teaching the people the laws of Moses.

● *Key point:*
With God's help, people can rebuild their lives even after the most tragic experiences.

● *Author, date:*
Unknown. Jewish tradition says the priest Ezra wrote it in the 400s BC, which is the setting of the story.

● *Main characters:*
Ezra, a priest who teaches the Jews
Cyrus, the Persian king who frees the Jews

● *Biggest scene:*
In the ruins of a once-beautiful Jerusalem, returning Jewish exiles begin rebuilding their city by laying the foundation for a new temple. Many shout for joy, but old priests, who remember Solomon's glorious temple, weep (Ezra 3:12–13).

● *Most famous line:*
'For He is good, For His mercy endures forever' (Ezra 3:11).

Nehemiah

● *In a paragraph:*
A servant in the Persian palace, Nehemiah gets the king's permission to take a leave of absence and rebuild Jerusalem's walls. Babylonian invaders had demolished the walls a century earlier. Despite opposition from non-Jewish locals, who didn't want the Jews to regain a foothold in the region, Nehemiah's crew finishes the work in an astonishing 52 days. Afterwards, the priest

Ezra reads from the Law of Moses – perhaps from Deuteronomy – and then leads the people in pledging their allegiance to God.

● **Key point:**
Faith and action go hand in hand: 'We prayed to our God and guarded the city day and night to protect ourselves' (Nehemiah 4:9).

● **Author, date:**
Unknown. Jewish tradition says Ezra wrote it in the 400s BC, which is when the story took place.

● **Main characters:**
Nehemiah, a Jew who leads the rebuilding of Jerusalem's walls
Sanballat, a non-Jew who tries to stop the rebuilding
Ezra, a priest who reads the Jewish law to the people

Cyrus on the record

The clay Cylinder of Cyrus pictured below confirms the book of Ezra's report that the Persian King Cyrus freed the Jewish exiles to go home. Dating from 536 BC – during Cyrus' reign – this cylinder says the king freed all people who had been exiled from their homelands by the Babylonians, the world's former superpower recently defeated by Persia.

● **Biggest scene:**
Fearing attack from non-Jews in the area, the Jews rush to repair Jerusalem's walls – keeping one hand free to grab a weapon and fight if necessary. Working from sunrise to sunset, they finish the work in less than two months (Nehemiah 6).

● **Most famous line:**
'Those who carried materials did their work with one hand and carried a weapon with the other.' (Nehemiah 4:17)

Esther

● *In a paragraph:*

Mordecai, a Jew in Persia – now Iran – refuses to bow to a top palace official, Haman. In retaliation, Haman decides to wipe out all Jews and confiscate their property – not realizing that Queen Esther is both a Jew and Mordecai's cousin. He gets an irrevocable decree from the king to conduct an empire-wide holocaust, without bothering to identify the race of people. Persuaded by Mordecai, Esther reveals her Jewish identity and convinces the king to issue a counter-decree allowing Jews to protect themselves, aided by Persian soldiers. The king executes Haman and gives his job to Mordecai.

● *Key point:*

Though God's name isn't mentioned in the story, he's at work behind the scenes, protecting his people by placing a Jewish queen on the throne at just the right time.

● *Author, date:*

Unknown. The story takes place in the 400s BC.

● *Main characters:*

Esther, the Jewish queen of Persia
Xerxes, the king of Persia
Mordecai, Queen Esther's cousin who raised her
Haman, an official intent on killing all Jews

● *Biggest scene:*

During a royal banquet that Haman thinks Queen Esther is giving to honour him, she reveals that she is a Jew – and therefore a target of Haman's holocaust. 'My people and I have been sold to those who would kill, slaughter, and annihilate us' (Esther 7:4). Haman is shocked – and then hanged.

● *Most famous line:*

'You may have been chosen queen for just such a time as this' (Esther 4:14).

Job

● *In a paragraph:*
God agrees to let Satan test the faith of a righteous man named Job. Raiders steal Job's herds and kill his servants. A windstorm kills his children, crushing a house where they're eating. Boils erupt all over his body. Friends come and advise him to repent, arguing that he must have done something terrible to deserve this. Job insists that he's innocent, and he demands an explanation from God. Instead, God convinces Job to trust him no matter what. Then God restores Job's health and wealth, and gives him more children.

● *Key point:*
Though many Jews in biblical times believed that tragedies are caused by sin, Job's story teaches otherwise.

● *Author, date:*
Unknown, though clues in the story suggest the writer is a Jew telling a story from around the time of Israel's founding fathers – roughly 2000 BC.

● *Main character:*
Job, a rich herder who loses his wealth, children, and health

● *Biggest scene:*
Sitting with friends who have come to comfort him, but instead accuse him of committing some unconfessed sin, Job fires back: 'What miserable comforters you are!' (Job 16:2).

● *Most famous line:*
'The Lord gave, and the Lord has taken away; Blessed be the name of the Lord.' (Job 1:21)

Iraqi Job

There's another ancient story of a righteous man suffering – this one from humanity's first known civilization, Sumer, in what was Abraham's homeland in southern Iraq. Written before 2000 BC, the story features a man whom scholars sometimes call 'Sumerian Job'.

Like Job in the Bible, Sumerian Job suffers unfairly and complains bitterly.

Sumerian Job: 'Let my mother who gave birth to me not stop weeping for me.'
Bible Job: 'Why didn't I die as soon as I was born?' (Job 3:11)

In the end, both come to trust God.

Sumerian Job: 'I have set my sights on you as on the rising sun.'
Bible Job: 'I take back everything I said, and I sit in dust and ashes to show my repentance' (Job 42).

Musicians playing a flute and a lyre, which is a small harp.

Psalms

● **In a paragraph:**

A Jewish songbook, Psalms is a collection of poetry spanning centuries. Surprisingly, there are more complaint psalms than any other kind. But there are also many songs of thanks to God, which is why Jews call this book *Tehillim*, which is Hebrew for 'praises.' Set to music, Jews sang the words at home, on the road during pilgrimages to Jerusalem, and at worship in the temple.

● **Key point:**

We can be honest with God – expressing any feeling we have: anger, fear, disappointment, confusion. Psalms contains them all.

● **Author, date:**

Various writers over many centuries. Seventy-three songs are attributed to David, but in a vague reference that could mean the songs were written by him, inspired by him, or dedicated to him. Other songs are associated with Solomon, Moses and Asaph, a music leader in David's time.

● **Main character:**

David, the source or inspiration behind almost half of the 150 songs

---

Poetic thoughts instead of sounds

Ancient Hebrew poems didn't rhyme, as many poems do today. Instead of repeating sounds, Hebrew poets repeated or compared thoughts. One line might repeat, contrast or extend an idea from an earlier line. In the following passage, the second line repeats the thought of the first:
'O Lord, why do you stand so far away?
Why do you hide when I need you the most?' (Psalm 10:1)

● *Biggest scene:*
When God's people face grave danger, God leads them just as a
shepherd leads his flock. 'Even when I walk through the dark
valley of death, I will not be afraid, for you are close beside me.
Your rod and your staff protect and comfort me.' (Psalm 23:4)

● *Most famous line:*
'The Lord *is* my shepherd; I shall not want. He makes me to lie
down in green pastures; He leads me beside the still waters'
(Psalm 23:1–2).

Proverbs

● *In a paragraph:*
King Solomon and other wise men from Israel offer the
wisdom of their experience in a collection of sayings targeted
especially at young men. Short and snappy, most of these
proverbs are two-liners – making them easy to remember.
Topics cover a wide array of spiritual and practical matters,
including sex, money and raising children.

● *Key point:*
'The purpose of these proverbs is to teach people wisdom and
discipline… Through these proverbs, people will receive
instruction in discipline, good conduct, and doing what is
right, just, and fair. These proverbs will make the simple-
minded clever. They will give knowledge and purpose to
young people' (Proverbs 1:2–4).

● *Author, date:*
Various wise men over many centuries. Most are attributed to
Solomon, who wrote 3,000 in his lifetime (1 Kings 4:32).

● *Main character:*
Solomon, the wisest king of Israel and the source of most of
the book's proverbs

Biggest scene:
An immoral woman tries to seduce a young man away from his wife.
The sage's advice to the man: 'Stay away… Save yourself for your
wife and don't have sex with other women' (Proverbs 5:8, 17).

● *Most famous line:*
'Train up a child in the way he should go, And when he is old he will not depart from it' (Proverbs 22:6).

Ecclesiastes

● *In a paragraph:*
The writer, a deep thinker, explores the meaning of life. His initially bleak conclusion is: everything humans do is meaningless. We work, we die, and then life goes on without us. The wise, the rich and the pleasure-seeker all end up the same way – dead. Life is short, he concludes. So people should enjoy their blessings: food, family, and a job they love. 'Enjoy your work and accept your lot in life – that is indeed a gift from God' (Ecclesiastes 5:19).

● *Key point:*
'I have thought deeply about all that goes on here in the world... Here is my final conclusion: Fear God and obey his commands' (Ecclesiastes 8:9; 12:13).

● *Author, date:*
'These are the words of the Teacher, King David's son, who ruled in Jerusalem' (Ecclesiastes 1:1). Perhaps Solomon, writing in the 900s BC.

● *Main character:*
Teacher, a cryptic name given to the writer, supposedly Solomon

● *Biggest scene:*
The writer spins a wonderful poem about the seasons of life. 'There is a time for everything, a season for every activity under heaven. A time to be born and a time to die. A time to plant and a time to harvest' (Ecclesiastes 3:1–2).

● *Most famous line:*
'Eat, drink, and be merry' (Ecclesiastes 8:15).

Song of Songs

● *In a paragraph:*

In an erotic celebration of love, a man and a woman express their most intimate feelings for each other. Without crudeness, and yet with uninhibited sensuality, they speak frankly of their sexual desires for each other. But their love is deeper than flesh and more lasting than the moment. In an expression of commitment that many Bible experts say is the high point of this poem, the woman tells her beloved, 'Always keep me in your heart and wear this bracelet to remember me by' (Song of Songs 8:6).

● *Key point:*

Sexuality, in words and action, is a gift from God. It's a way to express our most intimate feelings to the one we promise to love for a lifetime.

● *Author, date:*

Called a song of Solomon, the Hebrew phrasing is such that the song could have been written by him, for him, or dedicated to him. Solomon lived in the mid-900s BC.

● *Main characters:*

Unidentified woman, from the countryside of Israel
Unidentified man, who is the woman's true love

● *Biggest scene:*

Either anticipating a honeymoon, or already enjoying it, the man sensually and lovingly expresses his desire: 'You are tall and slim like a palm tree, and your breasts are like its clusters of dates… I will climb up into the palm tree and take hold of its branches' (Song of Songs 7:7–8).

● *Most famous line:* 'Your love is sweeter than wine' (Song of Songs 1:2).

Isaiah

● *In a paragraph:*

During a dramatic vision, Isaiah sees God on his heavenly throne and is given the job of warning the Israelites. Isaiah's message: because of the people's persistent sin, both Israelite nations will collapse – Israel in the north, and Judah (his home) in the south. Isaiah lives to see the Assyrians overrun Israel and exile the survivors. Around 150 years later, the Babylonians do the same to Judah. Though Isaiah predicts that Israel will be wiped off the map, he says that's not the end of their story. God will bring them home and let them start again – cured of their attraction to idols, and finally devoted to him.

● *Key point:*

Though God is patient, he eventually punishes people if they continue sinning. But even after the punishment, there is love and mercy waiting.

● *Author, date:*

Isaiah, who ministered from around 740–700 BC. Some say he wrote only the first 39 chapters, which are set in his day, and that chapters 40–66 – set a century or more later – were written by someone else. Others say Isaiah predicted those events.

● *Main characters:*

Isaiah, a prophet in Jerusalem during the reigns of four kings

Hezekiah, one of the Israelite kings Isaiah advised

The Fifth Gospel

Some 700 years before Jesus was born, the prophet Isaiah wrote as if he knew him.

New Testament writers saw Jesus so clearly in Isaiah's prophecies that they quoted his book more than any other – about 50 times. Some scholars have even nicknamed Isaiah's book 'The Fifth Gospel'.

In one of the most familiar prophecies picked up by New Testament writers, Isaiah said, 'Look! The virgin will conceive a child! She will give birth to a son and will call him Immanuel – "God is with us"' (Isaiah 7:14).

This painting by Antonella da Messina depicts the suffering Christ.

● **Biggest scene:**

A suffering servant – interpreted by New Testament writers as Jesus – is punished for the sins of others. 'He was wounded and crushed for our sins. He was beaten that we might have peace... who among the people realized that he was dying for their sins – that he was suffering their

A copy of Isaiah's scroll, discovered among the famous Dead Sea Scrolls. Because Isaiah wrote about Jesus like an eyewitness, some wondered if the book was written after Jesus, making it history instead of prophecy. But this copy of the scroll dates a century before Jesus.

punishment? He had done no wrong, and he never deceived anyone. But he was buried like a criminal; he was put in a rich man's grave' (Isaiah 53:5, 8–9).

● *Most famous line:*

'For unto us a Child is born, Unto us a Son is given; And the government will be upon His shoulder. And His name will be called Wonderful, Counsellor, Mighty God, Everlasting Father, Prince of Peace' (Isaiah 9:6).

Jeremiah

● *In a paragraph:*
God calls a young priest – Jeremiah – to deliver the worst news
in Israelite history: their nation will be wiped off the map. The
northern nation of Israel is already gone, overrun by the
Assyrians. Jeremiah's warning jars the people of the southern
nation of Judah, and King Josiah leads a spiritual reform. But
when Josiah's gone, the people go back to ignoring God's laws
and worshipping idols. Against Jeremiah's recommendation,
King Zedekiah rebels against Babylon – the superpower that
imposes taxes on smaller nations. Babylon levels the walled cities
of Judah, including Jerusalem. Then the invaders exile most
survivors to what is now Iraq. Jeremiah is spared, because he had
advised Judah to surrender. But a group of Jews forces him to flee
with them to Egypt, where he is never heard from again.

● *Key point:*
Sin leads to punishment. But punishment doesn't mark the end
of God's love. He promises to restore Israel.

● *Author, date:*
Jeremiah dictated the book to his assistant, Baruch. Jeremiah
prophesied from 627–586 BC.

● *Main characters:*
Jeremiah, a prophet who sees Jerusalem destroyed
Jehoiakim, a king who burned Jeremiah's first prophecy,
which Jeremiah rewrote
Zedekiah, the last king of Judah

● *Biggest scene:*
After a siege lasting a year and a half, Babylonian soldiers break
through Jerusalem's city walls and slaughter the starving people
inside. Stone by stone, the Babylonians dismantle this last
Jewish city and then exile the survivors. The nation of Israel no
longer exists.

● *Most famous line:*
'Can a leopard change his spots?' (Jeremiah 13:23)

Baruch was here

Archaeologists seem to have found a clay impression of the very seal used by Jeremiah's secretarial scribe, Baruch. The seal, bearing Baruch's name, was pressed onto plugs of soft clay that sealed shut any of the scrolls he wrote on. This insured privacy, as a reader had to break the seal to read the scroll.

The impression that dates to Jeremiah's time reads: 'Belonging to Baruch, son of Neriah, the scribe.' The Bible, too, identifies Jeremiah's assistant as 'Baruch son of Neriah' (Jeremiah 32:12). Remarkably, there are even whirls of a fingerprint on the clay – perhaps Baruch's.

Lamentations

● *In a paragraph:*

The saddest book in the Bible, Lamentations is a collection of blues songs – bitter laments written by a man who witnessed the most tragic event in ancient Israel's history. It's an event that rivals the Holocaust in heartbreak. Invading Babylonians burn and level cities of the Jewish homeland – Jerusalem included. Survivors are led into exile in Babylon. The Jewish nation no longer exists. The writer watches it all, and cries until his eyes are red. Then he prays for God to restore the nation.

● *Key point:*

The Jews have suffered grief from beginning to end many times over. This is made clear by the message as well as the structure of the message. Most chapters contain 22 verses – the length of the Hebrew alphabet. Each verse starts with a different letter of the alphabet, beginning with *aleph*, followed by *beth*, and working through the alphabet. Grief, from beginning to end.

● *Author, date:*

Unknown. Ancient Jewish tradition says the prophet Jeremiah wrote it, as he was in Jerusalem when invaders overran it.

● *Main character:*

Unidentified narrator, an eyewitness to the fall of Jerusalem

● *Biggest scene:*
Babylonian soldiers surround Jerusalem and lay siege to it for what scholars estimate was two and a half years. Inside, starvation turns the people into animals. 'Mothers eat their little children, those they once bounced on their knees' (Lamentations 2:20).

● *Most famous line:*
'Great is thy faithfulness' (Lamentations 3:23).

Ezekiel

● *In a paragraph:*
A young Jerusalem priest named Ezekiel, along with other upper-class Jews, is deported to Babylon in what is now Iraq. Without a temple to minister in, Ezekiel can't function as a priest. But God calls him as a prophet, instructing him to predict the end of the Jewish nation. After Jerusalem falls, God gives him a new message to deliver – the restoration of Israel. 'I [will] bring them home from the lands of their enemies' (Ezekiel 39:27).

● *Key point:*
With God, there is hope in the most hopeless situations.

● *Author, date:*
'Ezekiel son of Buzi, a priest... in the land of the Babylonians' (Ezekiel 1:3). He served as a prophet for some twenty years, from around 593–571 BC.

● *Main character:*
Ezekiel, a priest and prophet

● *Biggest scene:*
In a vision, Ezekiel is transported to a valley filled with the dry

A new contract with God

It's not all doom that Jeremiah predicts. There's hope, too.

In time, God will allow the Jews to return to their homeland and rebuild it.

God will also make a new agreement with them – replacing the hundreds of old laws that were so hard to keep:

'I will put my laws in their minds, and I will write them on their hearts. I will be their God, and they will be my people. And they will not need to teach their neighbours... saying, "You should know the Lord." For everyone, from the least to the greatest, will already know me.' (Jeremiah 31:33–34)

New Testament writers said Jesus introduced that new covenant, making obsolete the old laws of Moses which many Jews still observe today, and opening the door of salvation to everyone.

bones of human beings. It looks as if a massacre took place there. Suddenly, a rattling sound fills the valley. Bones snap together; muscles and skin grow over them. Then a wind blows life into the corpses. 'These bones represent the people of Israel,' God says. 'O my people, I will open your graves of exile and cause you to rise again' (Ezekiel 37:11–12).

● *Most famous line:*
'Dry bones, hear the word of the Lord' (Ezekiel 37:4).

Daniel

● *In a paragraph:*
The world's new superpower, Babylon, discourages rebellion by deporting the smartest people in subordinate nations to Babylon – young Daniel among them. Daniel serves with distinction as an adviser to the Babylonian kings, and then to the Persians who conquer Babylon. His specialties are interpreting dreams and predicting the future. The last half of the book contains Daniel's bizarre dreams that seem to point to the end of human history. It concludes with the Bible's first explicit mention of life after death, which promises eternal life.

● *Key point:*
God is in control, even when it looks as if everything is falling apart. He will put the shattered pieces of Israel back together.

● *Author, date:*
Unknown. The writer may have been Daniel or someone who compiled the stories and prophecies about him. Daniel was taken captive around 605 BC and served as a palace adviser for more than 60 years.

One of ancient Babylon's entry gates, reconstructed in Iraq. Babylon, near modern-day Baghdad, was once capital of the Babylonian Empire, which dominated the Middle East.

● *Main characters:*

Daniel, a Jewish noble and prophet deported to Babylon

Shadrach, Meshach, Abednego, Daniel's colleagues, who survive an attempt to execute them in a furnace for refusing to worship an idol

Nebuchadnezzar, Babylon's most powerful king who exiles Daniel and friends from their Jewish homeland

● *Biggest scene:*

Daniel spends the night in a lion's den as punishment for praying to God instead of the king. Palace officials, jealous of

Daniel's power, concocted this plan to get rid of him by convincing the king to order everyone to pray to him for a month, or face hungry lions. Daniel survives the night, protected by an angel of God. The king, angry at the officials who had manipulated him, has them and their families thrown to the lions (Daniel 6).

● *Most famous line:*
'My God sent his angel to shut the lions' mouths' (Daniel 6:22).

Hosea

● *In a paragraph:*
God tells the prophet Hosea to marry a prostitute called Gomer, to illustrate a point. It's a bit like a parable, except that this story is real. The northern nation of Israel is on the verge of being wiped out by invaders, as punishment from God for centuries of idolatry. Gomer represents Israel, a nation committing spiritual adultery. Hosea represents God. Gomer gives birth to three children, perhaps none of whom are fathered by Hosea. Then she leaves Hosea, returning to prostitution. At God's command, Hosea buys her back from her new master. This, too, is a symbol: If Israel repents, God will forgive her, 'and my love will know no bounds' (Hosea 14:4).

● *Key point:*
It is never too late to ask God for forgiveness. And when we ask for it, we get it.

● *Author, date:*
Hosea, who prophesied from around 750–722 BC, until Assyria overran Israel

● *Main characters:*
Hosea, a prophet in the northern nation of Israel
Gomer, Hosea's wife, a former prostitute

● *Biggest scene:*
A godly prophet marries a prostitute, acting on this instruction from God: 'Go and marry a prostitute, so some of her children

will be born to you from other men. This will illustrate the way my people have been untrue to me, openly committing adultery against the Lord by worshipping other gods' (Hosea 1:2).

● *Most famous line:*
'They sow the wind, and reap the whirlwind' (Hosea 8:7).

Joel

● *In a paragraph:*
Locusts invade Israel and devastate the land, devouring crops and wild plants, and even stripping bark off the trees. Without shade, rivers and ponds dry up. Famine sets in. The prophet Joel uses this disaster as an object lesson to warn of an even more destructive invasion: 'The day of the Lord is upon us... a mighty army appears!' (Joel 2:1–2). The invasion is God's punishment for the nation's sin. But which invasion? Assyria in the 700s BC? Babylon in the 500s BC? Alexander the Great in the 300s BC? Whichever one it is, Joel says it's not too late to repent and be spared.

● *Key point:*
On what Joel calls the 'day of the Lord,' God is going to step into human history. In times past, this was a good thing because God helped the Israelites. But in the future, this will be disastrous because God is coming to punish the Israelites if they don't repent.

● *Author, date:*
Joel, son of Pethuel. The Bible reveals nothing else about him, or when he lived.

● *Main character:*
Joel, a Jewish prophet warning of a military invasion

● *Biggest scene*
'A vast army of locusts has invaded my land. It is a terrible army, too numerous to count! Its teeth are as sharp as the teeth of lions! They have destroyed my grapevines and fig trees, stripping their bark and leaving the branches white and bare' (Joel 1:6–7).

● *Most famous line:*
'Beat your plowshares into swords and your pruning hooks into spears' (Joel 3:10).

Amos

● *In a paragraph:*
God calls on Amos, a shepherd and fig grower in the southern nation of Judah, to deliver a stern warning to the prosperous nation of Israel in the north: stop exploiting the poor. Rich people sell poor people into slavery to recoup debts as small as the price of a sandal. And judges take bribes. The Israelites only go through the motions of religion – their rituals lack sincerity. If this doesn't change immediately, Amos says, God will destroy the nation. Amos may have lived to see just that, when Assyria decimated Israel in 722 BC.

● *Key point:*
Prosperity is no sign of God's favour. Sometimes it's just a sign of exploitation. For exploiters, Amos has a one-sentence warning – see 'Most famous line'.

● *Author, date:*
Amos, in the mid-700s BC

● *Main character:*
Amos, a shepherd and fig grower

● *Biggest scene:*
'Fat cows of Samaria' – women who oppress the poor and then ask their husbands for another drink – are taken captive by invaders and led away with barbs through their noses, 'like a fish on a hook!' (Amos 4:1, 2)

● *Most famous line:*
'Prepare to meet your God' (Amos 4:12).

Obadiah

In a paragraph:
Babylonian soldiers invade the southern nation of Judah and begin demolishing one city after another – ending with the capital, Jerusalem. Some refugees run for their lives to Edom, in what is now Jordan. But the people there hate the Jews, so they turn them over to the invaders. The prophet Obadiah says the Jews will one day return like a fire, setting Edom ablaze, 'devouring everything and leaving no survivors' (Obadiah 18).

● Key point:
The way we treat others is the way we can expect God to treat us.

● Author, date:
Obadiah, a prophet who ministered sometime before Babylon destroyed Judah in 586 BC. *Obadiah* means 'servant of the Lord'. That leads some scholars to speculate that this wasn't the writer's name, but a description of an unidentified prophet.

● Main character:
Obadiah, a prophet who predicts the fall of Edom and the return of Israel

● Biggest scene:
Jewish refugees run from an invading army, only to be greeted by a neighbouring nation cackling with delight over the Jewish tragedy. Those neighbours murder some of the Jews and arrest others, turning them over to the invaders, stealing their property and looting their homes (Obadiah 13–14).

● Most famous line:
'As you have done, it shall be done to you' (Obadiah 15).

Jonah

● In a paragraph:
God sends a Jewish prophet named Jonah on a frightful mission. Jonah is to deliver a warning to Nineveh, the capital of Assyria – one of the most vicious empires in human history. This is the empire that a few decades later would level Israel's

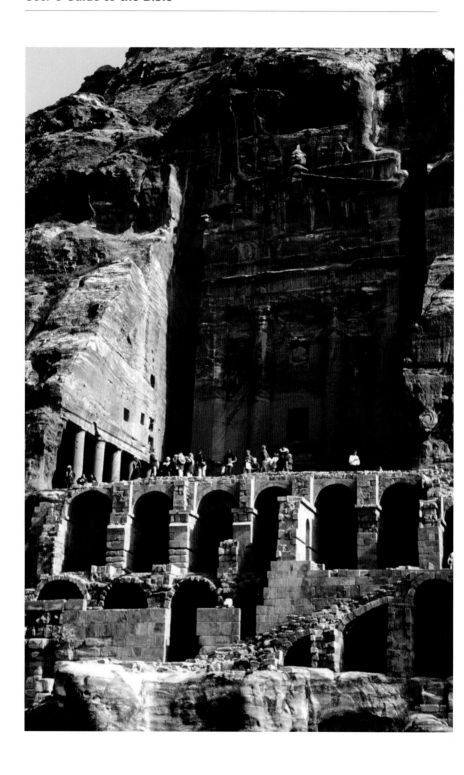

cities. Jonah's warning: Nineveh is about to be destroyed. Rather than deliver this message, and risk execution, Jonah booked passage on a ship headed in the opposite direction. God sends a storm to stop him. With Jonah's permission the crew throws Jonah overboard to calm the sea. A fish swallows Jonah and spews him up onto the shore. Jonah delivers the message to Nineveh and the people repent. So God spares the city.

● *Key point:*
God loves everyone, even the world's worst sinners who don't love him.

● *Author, date:*
'Jonah, son of Amittai' or perhaps someone telling his story for him. Though some say the story is a parable, the Bible elsewhere says this same prophet ministered in the northern nation of Israel during the 700s BC (2 Kings 14:25).

● *Main character:*
Jonah, a Jewish prophet sent on a mission to Nineveh in what is now Iraq

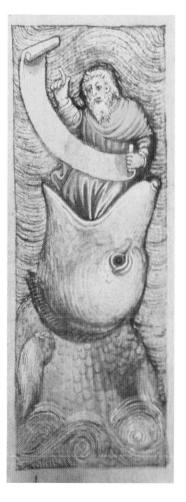

● *Biggest scene:*
A gale-force storm threatens to sink a ship, so the sailors throw a sacrifice into the sea: Jonah. He goes willingly because he knows he's the cause of the storm. A huge fish of some kind swallows him, carries him to shore and spits him out (Jonah 1).

Now a ghost town visited by tourists, Petra in modern-day Jordan was once the capital of Edom – a nation that betrayed the Jews to invaders.

● *Most famous line:*
'Jonah was inside the fish for three days and three nights' (Jonah 1:17).

Micah

● *In a paragraph:*
A small-town prophet takes on the rich and powerful of both Israelite nations – Israel in the north and Judah in the south. He delivers scathing rebukes from God, criticizing the rich for butchering the poor, judges for taking bribes, prophets for selling their words for profit, and the masses for worshipping idols. For this and more, Micah warns, God will wipe out both nations. But in time, Micah adds, God will restore the Jewish people to their homeland and all wars will stop.

● *Key point:*
Sin causes suffering, punishment and death. But even after the worst that sin can do, God still extends forgiveness, mercy and restoration to those willing to accept it.

● *Author, date:*
'Micah of Moresheth' (Micah 1:1), a prophet who lived through the reigns of three kings who ruled for a total of 55 years: 742–678 BC.

● *Main character:*
Micah, a rural prophet who lived a day's walk from Jerusalem

● *Biggest scene:*
A ruler is born in Bethlehem – a prophecy that Jews came to believe is about the promised messiah who will one day save Israel. 'He will stand to lead his flock with the Lord's strength... he will be highly honoured all around the world. And he will be the source of our peace' (Micah 5:4–5).

● *Most famous line:*
'All the nations will beat their swords into plowshares and their spears into pruning hooks' (Micah 4:3).

Nahum

● *In a paragraph:*
Around a century after the brutal Assyrian Empire wipes out the northern Israelite nation of Israel, Assyria continues to bully the southern nation of Judah and other Middle Eastern nations – forcing them to pay high taxes. That's when the prophet Nahum arrives with a message for them from God: 'I am preparing a grave for you because you are despicable and don't deserve to live!' (Nahum 1:14).

● *Key point:*
No power on earth is any match for God.

● *Author, date:*
Nahum, a prophet. He probably lived sometime in the half-century after Assyria conquered the Egyptian capital Thebes in 663 BC – as he mentions this – but before Babylon conquered Assyria in 612 BC – which he predicts.

● *Main character:*
Nahum, a prophet in the southern Israelite nation of Judah

● *Biggest scene:*
Nineveh, capital of the mighty Assyrian Empire – an empire stretching from what is now Iran and Turkey in the north-east to Egypt in the south-west – falls to an army of invaders. 'See the flashing swords and glittering spears in the upraised arms of the cavalry! The dead are lying in the streets – dead bodies, heaps of bodies, everywhere' (Nahum 3:3). Destined to emerge as the world's next superpower, Babylonian invaders swallow up the Assyrian territory.

● *Most famous line:*
'The Lord is slow to get angry, but his power is great, and he never lets the guilty go unpunished' (Nahum 3:1).

Habakkuk

● *In a paragraph:*
The Israelite prophet Habakkuk has a complaint for God: 'How long, O Lord, must I call for help? But you do not listen! "Violence!" I cry, but you do not come to save' (Habakkuk 1:2–3). Habakkuk is talking about sin in his nation of Judah. When God replies, and says he's sending the Babylonian army to punish the Israelites, Habakkuk is stunned: the Babylonians are even worse sinners. Habakkuk can't understand why God would allow them to 'destroy people who are more righteous than they'. God assures Habakkuk that in time the Babylonians will face their own judgment day. Meanwhile, God challenges all righteous people to have faith in him. Habakkuk rises to that challenge, and pledges his loyalty to God.

● *Key point:*
In God we trust, no matter what happens.

● *Author, date:*
Habakkuk, a prophet who seems to have ministered sometime during the quarter-century after Babylon crushed Assyria in 612 BC, but before Babylon destroyed Jerusalem in 586 BC.

● *Main character:*
Habakkuk, an Israelite prophet who questions the fairness of God

● *Biggest scene:*
An invading army storms through the Israelites' homeland, killing people, destroying crops, plundering livestock and wealth. But Habakkuk holds tight to his faith in God: 'I will rejoice in the Lord!... The Sovereign Lord is my strength! He will make me as surefooted as a deer and bring me safely over the mountains' (Habakkuk 3:18, 19).

● *Most famous line:*
'The righteous will live by his faith' (Habakkuk 2:4).

Why do good people suffer?

The Bible doesn't answer that question.

Job asked it. And God replied, 'Who is this that questions my wisdom with such ignorant words?' (Job 38:2).

Habakkuk asked it. And God replied, 'Wait patiently' (Habakkuk 2:3).

The disciples asked it when they saw a man born blind, and figured his blindness was a punishment for sin. Jesus replied, 'It was not because of his sins or his parents' sins. He was born blind so the power of God could be seen in him' (John 9:3). Then Jesus healed him.

Zephaniah

● *In a paragraph:*

The prophet Zephaniah warns fellow citizens of the southern Jewish nation of Judah that God's patience is running out and he is about to punish them for their centuries of sin. And, in what reads like a message of apocalyptic doom, Zephaniah adds that the entire world will be destroyed. Some Bible experts, however, argue that Zephaniah was referring simply to the Jewish nation. In either case, doomsday isn't the last day. After the destruction, God will gather his scattered people and bring them home to 'live peaceful lives, lying down to sleep in safety' (Zephaniah 3:13).

● *Key point:*

God punishes rampant corruption and injustice, sometimes as dramatically as he did with the flood in Noah's time.

● *Author, date:*

The prophet Zephaniah, who probably lived a few decades before Babylon decimated Judah in 586 BC

● *Main character:*

Zephaniah, a prophet who predicts the destruction of Judah – and perhaps the rest of the world

● *Biggest scene:*

'I will sweep away everything from the earth,' says the Lord. 'I will sweep away the people and animals; I will destroy the birds in the air and the fish of the sea. I will ruin the evil people, and I will remove human beings from the earth' (Zephaniah 1:2–3). **77**

The order of destruction reverses the order of Creation in Genesis 1 – as though God is undoing Creation.

● *Most famous line:*
'Walk humbly and do what is right' (Zephaniah 2:3).

Haggai

● *In a paragraph:*
Around twenty years after the Jews return to their homeland from exile, they still haven't rebuilt the Jerusalem temple. Following a bad harvest in 520 BC, the prophet Haggai tells the people they can expect more crop failures until they get to work on the temple. They organize themselves right away. They start the project within three weeks and finish the foundation by winter. Elated, Haggai assures them of good crops in the seasons ahead. The temple is dedicated around three and a half years after the work starts.

● *Key point:*
God sometimes withholds blessing and prosperity from people as a way to get their attention. At other times, he pours out blessings as a reward. But this is not a universal law, as Job's story confirms.

● *Author, date:*
Haggai, a prophet who lived in the 500s BC, after the Jews returned from exile to rebuild their homeland

● *Main character:*
Haggai, who urges the Jews to rebuild the Jerusalem temple

● *Biggest scene:*
'You have planted much but harvested little. You have food to eat, but not enough to fill you up. You have wine to drink, but not enough to satisfy your thirst. You have clothing to wear, but not enough to keep you warm. Your wages disappear as though you were putting them in pockets filled with holes!' (Haggai 1:6)

● *Most famous line:*
'Why are you living in luxurious houses while my house [God's temple] lies in ruins?' (Haggai 1:3)

Zechariah

● *In a paragraph:*
Zechariah and Haggai are prophets living in Jerusalem at the same time, delivering similar messages. The Jews returned from exile eighteen years earlier, and have not yet rebuilt the temple – which is the only place where they are allowed to offer sacrifices in worship of God. Zechariah urges the people to rebuild both the temple and the rest of the city. He also calls them to righteousness, promising that, although God will punish the sinful, he will forgive the repentant. 'Return to me, and I will return to you, says the Lord Almighty' (Zechariah 1:3). Zechariah then closes his book with several chapters of prophecy about Israel's bright future, under the messiah's leadership.

● *Key point:*
'My Temple will be rebuilt, says the Lord Almighty… Israel will again overflow with prosperity' (Zechariah 1:16–17).

● *Author, date:*
'The prophet Zechariah son of Berekiah and grandson of Iddo' (Zechariah 1:1). Zechariah received messages from God in 520 BC, during the autumn of the second year of King Darius' reign.

● *Main character:*
Zechariah, a prophet and priest who urges people to finish rebuilding Jerusalem

● *Biggest scene:*
Sometime after Jerusalem is rebuilt, a unique king arrives, humble and riding on a donkey. 'Your king will bring peace to the nations. His realm will stretch from sea to sea… to the ends of the earth.' (Zechariah 9:10) New Testament writers said Jesus fulfilled this prophecy 500 years later.

● *Most famous line:*
'Shout in triumph, O people of Jerusalem! Look, your king is coming to you… he is humble, riding on a donkey' (Zechariah 9:9).

Malachi

● *In a paragraph:*

Perhaps a century after the Jews return from exile to rebuild their nation, they're starting to forget the main lesson the exile taught them: God punishes sin. Though they aren't worshipping idols – the main sin that got them exiled – they're ignoring many of God's other laws. They've stopped giving 10 per cent of their money to the temple. They're lying in court, exploiting the poor, and offering diseased animals for sacrifice.

● *Key point:*

God wants genuine worship that flows out of devotion and love. He's not interested in people merely going through the motions of mindless rituals.

When did Christians start tithing?

The shocking answer is in the 1800s.

The New Testament never mentions Christians tithing. And church leaders during the first centuries said Christians didn't tithe, they gave offerings. These leaders taught that tithing was part of the old, legalistic Jewish system – much like animal sacrifices, kosher food laws and circumcision – which they said became obsolete after Jesus set up a new covenant between humanity and God.

Christians originally weren't as financially pressured as they are today because they had no church buildings to support. That's because Rome outlawed Christianity, and believers met secretly in private homes. Only in the AD 300s, after Rome legalized Christianity, did believers start building churches.

From time to time church leaders in select areas of the world imposed a church tax on people, but it wasn't until the 1800s that preachers started insisting that there are biblical grounds for tithing. Church historians have been unable to find a single sermon on tithing before that, according to Dr Paul Merritt Bassett, Professor of the History of Christianity at Nazarene Theological Seminary.

In the 1800s, the church was just starting massive missionary campaigns, which needed funding. Some preachers responded by arguing that Old Testament laws about tithing weren't uniquely Jewish, but were moral laws that apply to everyone – like the Ten Commandments.

Even Christians who don't agree, however, understand that it takes money to keep the church doors open – and that 'God loves a cheerful giver' (2 Corinthians 9:7).

● *Author, date:*
Either a prophet named Malachi or an unidentified person using
the word *malachi* ('my messenger') as a general description. Clues
in the book suggest the writer lived in the 400s BC.

● *Main character:*
Malachi, a prophet condemning insincere worship in Israel

● *Biggest scene:*
Instead of obeying Jewish law by bringing the best animals they
have for sacrifice at the temple, many Jews bring the worst of
their flocks. Malachi delivers a stern rebuke from the Lord
Almighty: 'When you give blind animals as sacrifices, isn't that
wrong? And isn't it wrong to offer animals that are crippled and
diseased? Try giving gifts like that to your governor, and see how
pleased he is… I wish that someone among you would shut the
Temple doors so that these worthless sacrifices could not be
offered! I am not at all pleased with you' (Malachi 1:8, 10).

● *Most famous line:*
'The Sun of Righteousness will rise with healing in his wings'
(Malachi 4:2).

The Bible Jesus lived

God's new agreement

New Testament means 'new agreement' – as in a new covenant between God and humanity. The Old Testament deals with God's first covenant, which was with the Jews. The New Testament deals with God's final covenant, with all of humanity.

A quick peek

Picking up where the Old Testament leaves off, the 27 books of the New Testament were written by various authors over a stretch of around 50 years. The Jews are waiting for God to make a new agreement with them, to replace the old one that was based on animal sacrifices and hundreds of laws. They're also waiting for a new king – a *messiah* ('deliverer') – who will bring peace.

The New Testament introduces both. Jesus, the Prince of Peace, is the messiah. The first four books in the New Testament tell his story: Matthew, Mark, Luke, and John. They're called *Gospels*, from an Old English word meaning 'good news'.

Letters make up most of the rest of the New Testament – letters to congregations and individuals, written by church leaders such as Paul, Peter and John. These letters explain that the death and resurrection of Jesus mark the end of the old agreement between God and humanity. The sacrificial system has become obsolete because of the sacrifice Jesus made when he died on the cross. Jewish laws about how to live are no longer necessary because the Holy Spirit is available to everyone, and he teaches them right from wrong.

Highlights from the New Testament include:

● God sends his Son, Jesus, to teach people how to live as citizens of God's spiritual kingdom.

● Jesus takes the death penalty that humans deserve for their sins.

- Jesus rises from the dead, proving to his followers that there's life after death.

- Before returning to heaven, Jesus asks his followers to spread his teachings around the world.

- The Holy Spirit arrives, providing spiritual power and direction for Christians.

- Jews, and later non-Jews, join the new movement that produces the Christian church.

- Preachers and prophets urge Christians to live in peace and humility, while patiently waiting for Jesus to return.

New Testament library

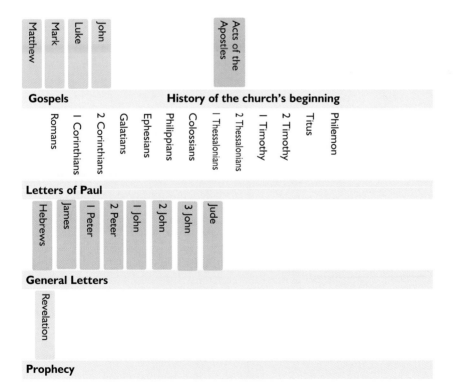

Matthew · Mark · Luke · John

Gospels

Acts of the Apostles

History of the church's beginning

Romans · 1 Corinthians · 2 Corinthians · Galatians · Ephesians · Philippians · Colossians · 1 Thessalonians · 2 Thessalonians · 1 Timothy · 2 Timothy · Titus · Philemon

Letters of Paul

Hebrews · James · 1 Peter · 2 Peter · 1 John · 2 John · 3 John · Jude

General Letters

Revelation

Prophecy

What's unique about Matthew?

By the book

Matthew

What's unique about Matthew?

Matthew is the most Jewish of the four gospels. That's why it's a perfect link between the Jewish Bible (the Old Testament) and the Christian New Testament. The Old Testament predicts the coming of a saviour, and Matthew reports his arrival. Matthew quotes the Jewish Bible more times than any other gospel, quoting nearly 60 prophecies and declaring Jesus the fulfilment of each one. The runner-up, Mark, cites only half as many prophecies.

● *In a paragraph:*

In Bethlehem, a virgin gives birth to a descendant of King David – just as Old Testament prophets had predicted. His name is Jesus, conceived by the Holy Spirit and born to Mary. An angel explains this to Mary's fiancé, Joseph, adding that this miraculous child, 'will save his people from their sins' (Matthew 1:21). Jesus is raised as a carpenter's son in Nazareth and then at the age of about 30 or more he launches his ministry of teaching and healing. His words and miracles are so compelling that crowds of Jews embrace him as the messiah whom the prophets had said would one day come to save Israel. Jewish scholars envy his popularity, and some fear he might lead a revolt that Rome will certainly crush – decimating the Jewish homeland in the process. So they secretly arrest him and convince the Roman governor to crucify him as a rebel. Jesus rises from the dead, and gives his followers an assignment that becomes known as the Great Commission: 'Go and make disciples of all nations' (Matthew 28:19).

● *Key point:*

Jesus is the messiah whom God had promised to send Israel, to save the people and rule them in peace. The Jews misunderstand God's promise because they think of the messiah only in political terms. But the salvation and peace Jesus offers exceeds their greatest expectations – extending into the spiritual world and enduring forever.

● *Author, date:*

Unknown. Early church leaders said it was written by Matthew, a tax collector who became one of Jesus' twelve disciples.

● *Main characters:*

Jesus, God's Son in a human body
Twelve disciples, followers of Jesus
Mary, the mother of Jesus
Joseph, Mary's husband and the legal father of Jesus
Pilate, a Roman governor who condemns Jesus to death

● *Biggest scene:*

Early on Sunday morning, grieving women go to Jesus' tomb to finish preparing his body for burial – only to find him alive and talking. 'Greetings,' he says. 'Don't be afraid!' (Matthew 28:9–10).

● *Most famous line:*

'Do to others what you would have them do to you' (Matthew 7:12).

When was Jesus born?

Strange as it may seem, Jesus was probably born sometime between 7–4 BC (Before Christ).

King Herod– who tried to kill young Jesus by ordering the slaughter of all Bethlehem boys aged two and under - died in 4 BC. If Herod died shortly after the slaughter, and Jesus was two years old by then, that would push the birth of Jesus back to 6 BC.

Today's calendar, established by Pope Gregory XIII in 1582 to honour Jesus, drew on mistaken calculations.

The star of Bethlehem

Matthew is the only Gospel that tells the story of wise men from the east – probably in what is now Iraq or Iran – following a star to Bethlehem.

Some ancient astrologers taught that the appearance of a new star marked the birth of a future king. And as this star seemed in some way to point to the Jewish homeland, the wise men concluded the child would become 'king of the Jews' (Matthew 2:2).

Most Bible scholars estimate Jesus was born sometime between 6–4 BC. Theories about what the star was include the following:

- A supernova reported by the Chinese in 5 BC.

- A conjunction of Jupiter (representing kings) and Saturn (representing Jews) in the constellation of Pisces (representing the land of Israel) in 7 BC.

- A spiritual being, perhaps similar to the pillar of fire that led Moses and the Israelites during the Exodus.

Sermon on the Mount

Jesus preached the most famous sermon in the Bible – the Sermon on the Mount.

The reason it's so famous is because it reads like a collection of his best teachings. Spanning Matthew chapters 5–7, the sermon includes many famous passages such as this:

'God blesses those who are merciful, for they will be shown mercy.' (Matthew 5:7)

This is just one prescription for spiritual happiness found in a collection of wise sayings called the Beatitudes.

'You are the light of the world… let your good deeds shine out for all to see, so that everyone will praise your heavenly Father.' (Matthew 5:14, 16)

'Love your enemies! Pray for those who persecute you!' (Matthew 5:44)

'Don't do your good deeds publicly, to be admired… Give your gifts in secret.' (Matthew 6:1, 4)

Pray like this: 'Our Father in heaven, Hallowed be Your name. Your kingdom come. Your will be done, On earth as it is in heaven.' (Matthew 6:9–10)

'Don't store up treasures here on earth… Store your treasures in heaven.' (Matthew 6:19–20)

Mark

● *In a paragraph:*

Mark is the shortest, fastest-paced and most action-packed of the four gospel stories about Jesus. Skipping slower-paced stories of Jesus' birth and childhood, the writer jumps right into the baptism that launched Jesus' career as a teacher and healer. Jesus hand-picks a dozen disciples to follow him and learn from him. Then he sets out on his life's work, which lasts only around three years. His teachings are so fresh and insightful, and his healing miracles are so astonishing that he draws crowds wherever he goes. Religious scholars who hate his non-traditional ideas try to discredit him by challenging him in public, but Jesus manages to humiliate them every time. So they stop debating him. Instead, they secretly arrest him, try him for teaching heresy, and convince the Romans to crucify him as a rebel who claims to be 'king of the Jews'. Jesus is nailed to a cross by 9 a.m. on Friday, is dead by about 3 p.m., and is buried by sundown. But he's alive again on Sunday morning.

page 86 After three years of ministry, Jesus is crucified. Jewish leaders condemned him to death for the blasphemy of claiming to be God's Son. Then they convinced the Roman governor to execute him as a rebel who claimed he was king of the Jews.

● *Key point:*

Jesus suffered for the sins of humanity, taking the punishment the people deserved – much as sacrificial animals once died to pay the penalty for the sins of worshippers.

87

What's unique about Mark?

The suffering of Jesus is Mark's special emphasis. There are only sixteen chapters in this short gospel, and the last six are devoted to Jesus' final week – now called Passion Week. *Passion* is an old word that used to mean 'suffering'.

If Mark's Gospel was written in the AD 60s, as many scholars suggest, the emphasis on suffering would have been especially relevant to believers. It was in AD 64 that Emperor Nero began persecuting Christians, after accusing them of starting the fire that destroyed two-thirds of Rome. This persecution continued off and on, depending on who was emperor, for almost three centuries.

● *Author, date:*

Unknown. Church leaders in the early AD 100s – a few decades after the gospel was written – said the writer was John Mark and that he based it on information from Peter, the leader of the disciples.

● *Main characters:*

Jesus, God's Son
Twelve disciples, followers of Jesus
Pilate, a Roman governor who condemns Jesus to death

Why did Jesus have to die?

Why couldn't God have come up with a less painful plan for saving humanity from sin? Why did he have to send his Son to be tortured and executed? It sounds so needlessly cruel. Couldn't an all-knowing God have done better?

When we boil down all the theological theories about why Jesus had to die, we're left with just that: theories. It's a mystery that we humans can't fully grasp. The Bible doesn't always explain the reasoning behind why God does what he does. It simply states it as a fact. Jesus 'died for our sins, just as God our Father planned, in order to rescue us from this evil world in which we live' (Galatians 1:4).

But we do know what Jesus' death accomplished. His crucifixion:

● Graphically shows how deadly serious sin is, from God's perspective. 'When people sin, they earn what sin pays – death' (Romans 6:23).

● Fulfilled the death penalty requirement for all sinners. 'God showed his great love for us by sending Christ to die for us while we were still sinners' (Romans 5:8).

● Set the stage for the Resurrection – which became convincing evidence that believers can put their lives on the line for God because death isn't the end. This gave the disciples – who hid during the crucifixion – the confidence to preach a few weeks later to Jerusalem crowds that included the same Jewish leaders who orchestrated Jesus' execution. And the church was born.

Coffin of Jesus' killer

Caiaphas' stone coffin, found buried in Jerusalem in 1990, contained the bones of a man aged about 60. Most scholars say this was probably the high priest who condemned Jesus to death. Though the Bible simply calls him Caiaphas, a first-century Jewish historian implied that this was a family name, and identified him more specifically as 'Joseph, who was called Caiaphas'. Engraved on the ornate coffin was: 'Joseph son of Caiaphas'.

● *Biggest scene:*
After an all-night, secret trial by the Jewish council – the highest authority in Jewish religion – Jesus is executed by the Romans, who reluctantly concede to Jewish demand. Nailed to a cross, Jesus is dead within six hours (Mark 15).

● *Most famous line:*
'Give to Caesar the things that are Caesar's, and give to God the things that are God's' (Mark 12:17).

Luke

● *In a paragraph:*
As God's angel Gabriel promised, Mary – still a virgin and engaged to Joseph – gives birth to Jesus, the Son of God. As a twelve-year-old youngster, Jesus impresses Jewish scholars with his understanding of scripture. But at the age of 30, after starting his ministry as a teacher and a miracle-working healer of the blind, crippled and deaf, scholars grow to hate him. He disagrees with many of their strict rules, which he says go way beyond what God intended. For example, they oppose healing people on the Sabbath, arguing that healing is 'work' and that God

What's unique about Luke?

Some of the Bible's most famous stories appear only in Luke. Among them are:

- Newborn Jesus lying in a manger

- Angels announcing Jesus' birth to shepherds in the field

- Parable of the Good Samaritan

- Parable of the Prodigal Son

- The widow who gave away her last 'mite', the smallest change of the day

created the Sabbath as a day of rest. Jesus asks what sense it makes to pull an animal out of a ditch on the Sabbath – which is considered acceptable – and yet refuse to help a sick person. Defenceless against Jesus' arguments, scholars decide to silence him. So to avoid starting a riot led by crowds who admire Jesus, the scholars secretly arrest him at night and then rush him through an all-night trial. Romans execute him the next morning – a Friday. But on Sunday morning, Jesus rises from the dead. During the next 40 days, he appears to many of his followers, calming their fears and preparing them to begin a new religious movement that will become known as Christianity.

● *Key point:*
Jesus is humanity's saviour. Matthew and Mark don't even use the word *saviour*. John uses it once. But Luke, thought to be non-Jewish, carefully selects stories that show salvation is for everyone – not just the Jews: 'I have seen the Saviour… given to all people. He is a light to reveal God to the nations' (Luke 2:30–32).

● *Author, date:*
Unknown. Church leaders in the AD 100s identified the writer as Luke, who they said also wrote a sequel: the early church history called Acts of the Apostles. Luke was Paul's associate – a physician Paul once described as 'Dear Doctor Luke' (Colossians 4:14).

● *Main characters:*
Jesus, God's Son
Twelve disciples, followers of Jesus
Mary, the mother of Jesus
Joseph, Mary's husband and Jesus' legal father
Pilate, a Roman governor who condemns Jesus to death

Jesus came to help powerless people, such as poor shepherds. Perhaps that's why God honoured shepherds by letting them be the first to visit baby Jesus.

● *Biggest scene:*
Born in what amounts to a barn – perhaps a cave where livestock are kept at night – the newborn Son of God lies in a feeding trough. His first visitors aren't royal dignitaries fit for a king, but lowly shepherds – society's powerless, like the people he came to serve.

● *Most famous line:*
'For unto you is born this day in the city of David a Saviour, which is Christ the Lord. And this shall be a sign unto you; Ye shall find the babe wrapped in swaddling clothes, lying in a manger' (Luke 2:11–12).

John

● *In a paragraph:*
Before starting his ministry, Jesus asks John the Baptist to baptize him. After this, Jesus selects a dozen disciples – working-class men instead of

Jesus in Roman history

A Roman Jew named Josephus – a historian born about seven years after the crucifixion – wrote about Jesus. Here are a few excerpts:

● 'There was a wise man who was called Jesus, and his conduct was good.'

● 'Pilate condemned him to be crucified and die.'

● 'His disciples... reported that he had appeared to them three days after his crucifixion.'

What's unique about John?

Radically unlike any of the other three gospel writers, John is driven by a single goal: to prove that Jesus is the divine Son of God. Jesus' teachings and miracles are carefully selected to help the reader come to this conclusion.

Bible experts don't even classify John with the other three, which are called Synoptic Gospels. *Synoptic* comes from a Greek word that means 'viewing together'. When we read the other three side-by-side, there are striking similarities. But John is incredibly different. Here are some key differences:

● John places Jesus at Creation, to emphasize his deity. Jesus is called the 'Word', a term Greek philosophers used to describe the cosmic reason behind the universe – a power that 'always exists' and through which 'all things happen'.

● There are only seven miracles, which the writer calls 'signs' – proofs of Jesus' divinity.

● Jesus describes himself with seven 'I am' statements, including 'I am the bread of life',

'the good shepherd' and 'the light of the world'. When Moses asked God for his name at the burning bush, God replied, 'I Am' (Exodus 3:14). So by adopting these 'I am' statements Jesus was clearly claiming to be God.

● Jesus' teachings and symbolism often work on many levels. When Jesus calls himself the 'bread of life', readers think of several images that apply:

Passover bread that the enslaved Israelites ate the night before they were freed from Egypt

manna that fell from heaven to keep them from starving in the desert

bread as their most basic food

communion bread that represented Jesus' broken body.

students of religion. He then launches into his mission of teaching and healing, which takes up the first half of the book. The closing half tells about Jesus' final week, beginning when he raises Lazarus from the dead. Afterwards, he rides into Jerusalem on a donkey, to the cheers of crowds who welcome him like a king: 'Praise God! Bless the one who comes in the name of the Lord! Hail to the King of Israel!' (John 12:13). This takes place on what later became known as Palm Sunday. Jewish leaders secretly arrest him on Thursday night because they're jealous of his popularity and they fear he might lead a doomed revolt against the Roman occupiers. They try him throughout the night. At daylight on Friday they take him to Pilate, the Roman governor, and pressure Pilate to order Jesus to be executed. Jesus is dead before sunset, but alive again on Sunday morning. This resurrection inspires the disciples to risk their own lives by spreading the good news about Jesus, for they finally realize the truth of what Jesus had been saying all along: 'Those who believe in me, even though they die like everyone else, will live again' (John 11:25).

● *Key point:*
'Believe that Jesus is the Messiah, the Son of God, and [that] by believing in him you will have life' (John 20:30).

● *Author, date:*
Unknown, but early church leaders said the gospel was written by one of Jesus' closest disciples: John, the brother of James and the son of Zebedee.

● *Main characters:*
Jesus, the divine Son of God
Twelve disciples, followers of Jesus
John the Baptist, a relative of Jesus who baptized him when Jesus began his ministry

● *Biggest scene:*
Mary Magdalene is crying outside the tomb of Jesus. She has come there with other women to finish preparing his body for burial, but the body is gone – stolen, she believes. As she weeps, she hears a familiar voice: 'Mary'. She turns and sees Jesus standing in front of her (John 20).

John the Baptist in Roman history

A Roman Jew called Josephus who wrote history in the first century said that many Jews believed that a ruler named Herod Agrippa lost an important battle 'as a punishment for what he did against John, who was called the Baptist: for Herod killed him, who was a good man who commanded the Jews to exercise virtue... and so to come to baptism.'

● *Most famous line:*
'God so loved the world that he gave his only Son, so that everyone who believes in him will not perish but have eternal life' (John 3:16). This verse is the entire story of Jesus condensed into one sentence – 'the Gospel in miniature' – according to Martin Luther, a priest who started the Protestant movement in the 1500s.

While Roman guards sleep outside Jesus' tomb, Mary Magdalene discovers that Jesus has risen from the dead.

Acts

● *In a paragraph:*

After spending several weeks with his disciples, the resurrected Jesus returns to heaven. But before he leaves, he tells the disciples to go to Jerusalem and wait for the Holy Spirit. The Spirit arrives and suddenly enables them to speak in languages they don't know. They go out among the crowds of Jews that have come to Jerusalem for a religious festival, and then begin preaching about Jesus and performing healing miracles. Three thousand people convert, and the Christian church is born. Jewish leaders persecute the Christians, even killing one called Stephen. Many flee the city, taking their new faith with them and spreading it to neighbouring regions. Paul, a former hard-line Jew, begins a more organized missionary movement – starting churches in cities throughout the Roman Empire. After about three decades, he is arrested and sent to Rome for trial before the emperor. Acts ends with Paul under arrest in Rome, where church leaders a century later said he was decapitated.

● *Key point:*
Through the power of the Holy Spirit, the church is born.

● *Author, date:*
Unknown. Church leaders in the AD 100s said the writer was Luke. They said he also wrote the prequel: the Gospel of Luke. Luke was Paul's associate – the physician Paul described as 'Dear Doctor Luke' (Colossians 4:14).

● *Main characters:*
Paul, a violent opponent of Christianity before becoming a convert and Christianity's first and most famous missionary
Peter, the leader of the Twelve disciples of Jesus
Barnabas, a church leader and missionary companion of Paul

● *Biggest scene:*
On his way to Damascus to arrest Jewish 'heretics' who believe Jesus is God's Son, Paul is blinded by a light from heaven. The voice of Jesus calls down, asking, 'Why are you persecuting me?' (Acts 9:4).

● *Most famous line:*
'You will be my witnesses in Jerusalem, and in all Judea and Samaria, and to the ends of the earth' (Acts 1:8).

The first 'Christians'

Converts to Christ's teachings weren't called 'Christians' until about a decade after Jesus' crucifixion. At first, believers called themselves followers of 'the Way' (Acts 24:14). It was at a church led by Paul and Barnabas in Antioch, Syria where 'believers were first called Christians' (Acts 11:26). The label may have been meant as an insult – like 'Moonies' for members of Sun Myung Moon's Unification Church.

PAUL'S THREE MISSIONARY JOURNEYS

During 20 years of missionary travels, Paul covered an estimated 16,000 kilometers (10,000 miles) starting churches throughout the Roman Empire.

On his first journey, commissioned by the church at Antioch and accompanied by Barnabas and Mark, he travelled to Cyprus and then to Asia Minor.

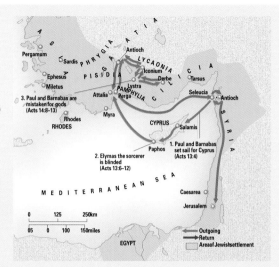

Paul took Silas on his second missionary journey. They revisited the Galatian churches and then went on to Greece, visiting Macedonia, Athens and then Corinth, where Paul stayed for two years.

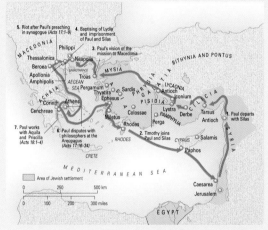

His third missionary journey took Paul to Ephesus, the principal city of the Roman province of Asia, where he built an important Christian church. From Ephesus, Christianity spread out across western Asia Minor.. Paul then returned home via Corinth to Jerusalem.

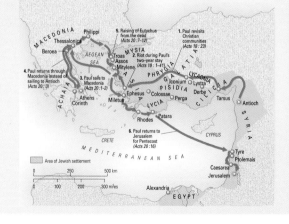

Romans

● In a paragraph:
This is Paul's most eloquent letter in the Bible, and it reads much like a theology professor explaining the basics of Christianity to new converts. After around twenty years of ministry and three church-planting missionary trips throughout the Roman Empire, Paul decides it's time to visit the Roman capital. So he writes this letter to Christians in Rome, introducing himself and summarizing his beliefs about the Christian faith. Paul says everyone has sinned, but that Jesus died to save us from our sins. All we have to do is believe that, and accept the free gift of God's salvation.

● Key point:
'If you confess with your mouth that Jesus is Lord and believe in your heart that God raised him from the dead, you will be saved' (Romans 10:9).

● Author, date:
The apostle Paul wrote this letter to Christians in Rome in about AD 57, near the end of his last missionary trip.

● Main character:
Paul, an ultra-conservative Jew (Pharisee) who converted to Christianity and became one of the most influential church leaders of all time, starting congregations throughout the Roman Empire

● Biggest scene:
The resurrected Jesus stands as a symbol of hope for humanity – of victory over sin and death. 'Just as Christ was raised from the dead by the glorious power of the Father, now we also may live new lives' (Romans 6:4).

Most famous line:
'All have sinned and fall short of the glory of God' (Romans 3:23).

Roman road to salvation

In his letters to Christians in Rome, Paul explains salvation this way:

● 'All have sinned; all fall short of God's glorious standard' (Romans 3:23).

● 'The wages of sin is death' (Romans 6:23).

● 'God showed his great love for us by sending Christ to die for us while we were still sinners' (Romans 5:8).

● 'It is by believing in your heart that you are made right with God, and it is by confessing with your mouth that you are saved' (Romans 10:10).

Pillars that once supported Apollo's temple stand in sad tribute to the once-thriving seaport town of Corinth, now a ruin of tumbled stone.

1 Corinthians

● In a paragraph:

Two or three years after starting the church in what is now Corinth, Greece, the apostle Paul gets a disturbing message. There are sharp divisions in the church over who's in charge. And there is continual arguing about a wide variety of topics. A sample includes: whether Christians should get married, whether they should eat meat dedicated to idols, how to dress for worship, how to observe the Lord's Supper (Communion), what to do about people flaunting their spiritual gifts – especially speaking in 'heavenly languages' – and how to discipline church members involved in sexual misconduct. In a practical, heartfelt letter, Paul addresses each of these problems, urging the church to stop fighting and to work together.

● *Key point:*
'Stop arguing among yourselves. Let there be real harmony so there won't be divisions in the church. I plead with you to be of one mind, united in thought and purpose' (1 Corinthians 1:10).

● *Author, date:*
Paul, writing around AD 55, two or three years after leaving Corinth

● *Main character:*
Paul, Christianity's first missionary, and the minister who started the church in Corinth

● *Biggest scene:*
Members of the Corinthian church are arguing about who their leader is. Some favour Paul. Others favour Peter, the leader of Jesus' disciples. Still others prefer a popular preacher named Apollos. 'My job was to plant the seed in your hearts,' Paul replied, 'and Apollos watered it, but it was God, not we, who made it grow... We work together as partners who belong to God. You are God's field... not ours' (1 Corinthians 3:6, 9).

● *Most famous line:*
'If I could speak in any language in heaven or on earth but didn't love others, I would only be making meaningless noise like a loud gong or a clanging cymbal' (1 Corinthians 13:1).

2 Corinthians

● *In a paragraph:*
Travelling preachers – Paul calls them 'false apostles' – arrive in Corinth and try to undermine his authority and take over. It's uncertain exactly what these intruders are saying about Paul. But based on his defence, they're saying he isn't a genuine apostle at all, but a self-appointed egomaniac who's out to get as much of their money as he can. Paul argues that the miracles he did among the Corinthians prove his work is of God. As for

99

ego, he says, 'We don't go around preaching about ourselves; we preach Christ Jesus' (2 Corinthians 4:5). And as for passing the collection plate, he reminds them that he supported himself in Corinth by making tents.

● *Key point:*
Paul defends himself as a genuine church leader. 'Please open your hearts to us. We have not done wrong to anyone. We have not led anyone astray. We have not taken advantage of anyone' (2 Corinthians 7:2).

● *Author, date:*
Paul, writing in about AD 55, just a few months after writing 1 Corinthians

● *Main character:*
Paul, the apostle who started the church in Corinth

● *Biggest scene:*
Paul suffers an incredible array of hardships because of his ministry: 'In everything we do we try to show that we are true ministers of God. We patiently endure troubles and hardships and calamities of every kind. We have been beaten, been put in jail, faced angry mobs, worked to exhaustion, endured sleepless nights, and gone without food' (2 Corinthians 6:4–5).

● *Most famous line:*
'God loves a cheerful giver' (2 Corinthians 9:7).

Paul's mysterious thorn in the flesh

'I was given a thorn in my flesh, a messenger from Satan to torment me and keep me from getting proud.'
(2 Corinthians 12:7)

Bible experts speculate this thorn may have been:

Physical, such as malaria that he picked up during a trip through Turkey's southern swampland.

Spiritual, such as sexual temptation, as he was unmarried.

Social, such as the worries that the Corinthians caused him.

Thorn isn't used anywhere else in the New Testament. But in the Old Testament, it refers to a group of people. Canaanites in Israel will become to the Jews 'thorns in your side' (Numbers 33:55).

Galatians

● *In a paragraph:*

God commissions Paul to preach to non-Jews, and to tell them they don't have to follow Jewish customs to worship God. Messianic Jews, who believe Jesus was the messiah, trail behind Paul and try to convince the converts that Paul is wrong. They insist that anyone who wants to be a Christian has to first become a Jew, and observe all Jewish traditions. Paul writes this emotionally charged letter denouncing that idea, and insisting that faith is all anyone needs for salvation. He uses Jewish history to illustrate his point, starting with Abraham, a faithful man whom God selected centuries before establishing the Jewish laws. Paul says the Jewish laws became obsolete with 'the coming of the child [Jesus]' (Galatians 3:19). Instead of living according to Jewish law, each Christian lives according to their 'new life in the Holy Spirit' (Galatians 5:16) – guided by laws written on the heart instead of laws written on scrolls.

> **Paul's harshest words**
>
> Frustration, throbbing with anger, comes through loud and clear in a single sentence Paul directed as his most persistent critics – Jews who insisted that any man who wanted to become a Christian needed to first become a Jew, and be circumcised. 'Why don't these agitators, obsessive as they are about circumcision, go all the way and castrate themselves!' (Galatians 5:12)

● *Key point:*

Christians are no longer required to obey the old Jewish laws from the time of Moses, such as laws about kosher food and circumcision.

● *Author, date:*

Paul wrote this letter, probably in the AD 50s, to churches throughout the Roman territory of Galatia, in what is now central Turkey.

● *Main characters:*

Paul, the apostle and missionary who worked mainly among non-Jews
Peter, a leading disciple and one who worked mainly among Jews

● *Biggest scene:*
The apostle Peter visits the church of Antioch, Syria – a congregation blended with Jews and non-Jews. Peter gets along fine with all of them until a delegation of Jerusalem Jews arrives. They convince him not to mix with the non-Jews, who are considered ritually unclean under old Jewish law. Paul, a bold advocate for the non-Jews, openly confronts Peter for this public offence: 'Why are you trying to make these Gentiles obey the Jewish laws you abandoned?' (Galatians 2:14).

● *Most famous line*: 'You reap whatever you sow' (Galatians 6:7)

Ephesians

● *In a paragraph:*
Sitting in jail, Paul writes a warm and encouraging letter to the congregation in what is now Ephesus, Turkey. He's not grappling with church problems, as he was in his letters to Corinth. Instead, he's giving his fellow Christians practical advice about how to live the Christian life – the kind of advice a pastor today might give in a sermon. Advice such as this:

'Let Christ be 'more and more at home in your hearts as you trust in him' (Ephesians 3:17).

'Be patient with each other, making allowance for each other's faults because of your love' (Ephesians 4:2).

'Throw off your old evil nature and your former way of life... You must display a new nature because you are a new person, created in God's likeness – righteous, holy, and true' (Ephesians 4:22, 24).

● *Key point:*
'Live a life filled with love for others, following the example of Christ, who loved you' (Ephesians 5:2).

● *Author, date:*
The apostle Paul wrote this letter while in jail, perhaps during his two-year arrest in Rome, which began around AD 60.

● *Main character:*
Paul, a travelling preacher who spent more than three years in Ephesus, helping to establish the church

● *Biggest scene:*
Christians suit up for spiritual warfare against 'evil rulers and authorities of the unseen world, against those mighty powers of darkness who rule this world, and against wicked spirits in the heavenly realms' (Ephesians 6:12). The spiritual armour includes truth, God's righteousness, peace that comes from Jesus' teachings, salvation, and the Spirit's guidance.

● *Most famous line:*
'Do not let the sun go down while you are still angry' (Ephesians 4:26).

Philippians

● *In a paragraph:*
From jail, Paul and his associate Timothy write this thank you letter to a church in what is now Philippi, Greece. The church has just sent gifts to the two men – perhaps warm clothing, money and food. There's a special bond between Paul and the people in this church. These Christians are the only ones – as far as the Bible reports – who were allowed to support Paul's ministry with money. Elsewhere, Paul supported himself as a bi-vocational pastor who made tents for a living. In addition to expressing gratitude for the gifts, Paul offers pastoral advice and encouragement, warning that the Philippian Christians may one day have to suffer for their faith, just as Paul and Timothy are doing now. In the meantime, he says, the Philippians should stick together, united in faith. 'Fix your thoughts on what is true and honorable and right... Keep putting into practice all you learned from me and heard from me and saw me doing, and the God of peace will be with you' (Philippians 4:8–9).

● *Key point:*
'Whatever happens to me, you must live in a manner worthy

of the Good News about Christ, as citizens of heaven' (Philippians 1:27).

● *Author, date:*

'This letter is from Paul and Timothy' (Philippians 1:1). They write from jail, perhaps during Paul's two-year arrest in Rome that began around AD 60.

● *Main character:*

Paul, a travelling minister who started the church in Philippi

Timothy, Paul's associate, also a minister.

● *Biggest scene:*

Drawing on an image from ancient Greek athletic competitions, Paul compares himself to a runner: 'I strain to reach the end of the race and receive the prize for which God, through Christ Jesus, is calling us up to heaven' (Philippians 3:14).

Greek runners in ancient competitions, straining to reach the finish line, provided Paul with an excellent illustration of the Christian life. For believers, Paul said, heaven is the prize.

● *Most famous line:*
'At the name of Jesus every knee will bow' (Philippians 2:10).

Colossians

● *In a paragraph:*
The apostle Paul gets word that some religious teachers have arrived in Colosse, and are spreading a distorted brand of Christianity. Paul didn't start the Colossian church, but one of his associates did. So he feels obligated to protect Christians there from what he calls 'empty philosophy and high-sounding nonsense that come from human thinking and from the evil powers of this world' (Colossians 2:8). The intruders accessorize Christianity with bits and pieces of Judaism and mystery cults from Rome. This produces a mutated teaching: faith in Jesus isn't enough for salvation – people also need to follow Jewish laws, deprive their body of comfort to learn self-discipline, and discover the secrets of God, which the teachers claim to have. Paul urges the Colossians to hold on to the teachings they received from his associate, and to 'Let the words of Christ, in all their richness, live in your hearts and make you wise' (Colossians 3:16).

● *Key point:*
Jesus is all anyone needs for salvation. 'You must continue to believe this truth and stand in it firmly' (Colossians 1:23).

● *Author, date:*
The apostle Paul writes this letter to Colosse, a church in western Turkey, signing it 'in my own handwriting – PAUL' (Colossians 4:18). He was in jail, perhaps during his two years of house arrest in Rome, beginning around AD 60.

● *Main character:*
Paul, a travelling minister whose associate started the church at Colosse.

● *Biggest scene:*
Paul pleads with Christians at Colosse to ignore false teachers. 'Don't let anyone condemn you for what you eat or drink, or

for not celebrating certain holy days... Don't let anyone condemn you by insisting on self-denial. And don't let anyone say you must worship angels, even though they say they have had visions about this' (Colossians 2:16, 18).

● *Most famous line:*
'Whatever you do, whether in word or deed, do it all in the name of the Lord Jesus' (Colossians 3:17).

1 Thessalonians

● *In a paragraph:*
On his second missionary trip, Paul hurriedly starts a church in Thessalonica, Greece and then moves on. He later gets a report that the new converts in Thessalonica are being persecuted, and that they want to know when Jesus will return. Paul writes this letter, reminding them that Jesus suffered, too. He tells them no one knows when Jesus will return – it will happen 'unexpectedly' (1 Thessalonians 5:2). But in the meantime, they should live like God's people – being honest, loving one another, minding their own business and working hard. 'As a

How to live the holy life

'Now may the God of peace make you holy in every way, and may your whole spirit and soul and body be kept blameless until that day when our Lord Jesus Christ comes again.' (1 Thessalonians 5:23).

That's Paul's prayer for believers in Thessalonica.
This prayer sounds very much like God's ancient command to everyone who wanted to be identified as his people: 'You must be holy because I am holy' (Leviticus 11:44).
But what does it mean to be holy? 'Perfect' doesn't seem to work because humans aren't perfect 'in every way'.
Here are a few theories:

● Holiness is a goal. As much as possible, we should try to model our lives after a perfect example: Jesus.

● It's possible to mature to a point that we no longer sin. That is, if we know something is wrong, we will choose not to do it. Only a tiny percentage of Christians seem to believe it's possible to continually overpower temptation.

● Holiness describes God as one-of-a-kind – transcendent and above everything in creation. People become holy when they serve him. Devoting themselves to this one-of-a-kind God transforms them into a one-of-a-kind people – a holy people whose lives begin to reveal that they are their Father's children.

result, people who are not Christians will respect the way you live' (1 Thessalonians 4:12).

● *Key point:*
'Live your lives in a way that God would consider worthy' (1 Thessalonians 2:12).

● *Author, date:*
'This letter is from Paul, Silas, and Timothy' (1 Thessalonians 1:1), although it's written in the first person, almost certainly by Paul. Written around AD 51, only about twenty years after Jesus' crucifixion, this is probably the oldest book in the New Testament.

● *Main characters:*
Paul, Christianity's most famous missionary, and the minister who started the church in Thessalonica, Greece
Timothy and Silas, close associates of Paul who later serve as pastors

● *Biggest scene:*
At the sound of a trumpet, Jesus returns to earth. 'First, all the Christians who have died will rise from their graves. Then, together with them, we who are still alive and remain on the earth will be caught up in the clouds to meet the Lord in the air and remain with him forever' (1 Thessalonians 4:16–17).

● *Most famous line:*
'The Lord will come like a thief in the night' (1 Thessalonians 5:2).

2 Thessalonians

● *In a paragraph:*
After getting Paul's first letter, which talks about Jesus' return, some Christians grow obsessed with the Second Coming. Some even stop working, and decide to live off the generosity of others until Jesus comes to take them to heaven. Paul jars them back to reality: 'Whoever does not work should not eat' (2 Thessalonians 3:10). Paul also urges the Thessalonians to stand firm in the face of persecution: 'Keep a strong grip on

everything we taught you both in person and by letter' (2 Thessalonians 2:15).

● *Key point:*
Jesus will return in his own good time. Meanwhile, keep living the Christian life and you can be assured of an eternal reward.

● *Author, date:*
Paul wrote this letter shortly after writing 1 Thessalonians, probably in AD 51–52.

● *Main character:*
Paul, founding minister of the church in Thessalonica, Greece

● *Biggest scene:*
Before Jesus returns, there is a great rebellion against God. 'The man of lawlessness is revealed – the one who brings destruction. He will exalt himself and defy every god there is and tear down every object of adoration and worship' (2 Thessalonians 2:3–4).

● *Most famous line:*
'Never get tired of doing good' (2 Thessalonians 3:13).

1 Timothy

● *In a paragraph:*
The apostle Paul writes this letter of practical advice to Timothy, an associate he has appointed to pastor the church at Ephesus, Turkey. Paul's advice covers many topics – all intended to help Timothy do a good job of leading the congregation in what is one of the largest cities in the Roman Empire. Topics include: prayer, women's roles in the church, what to look for in church leaders, how to deal with heretics and taking care of the poor.

● *Key point:*
'Pursue a godly life, along with faith, love, perseverance, and gentleness. Fight the good fight for what we believe. Hold tightly to the eternal life that God has given you' (1 Timothy 6:11–12).

● *Author, date:*
The letter claims to be from Paul. But because of a unique writing style and a different way of using some important words (like 'faith'), some scholars today wonder if a student of Paul's wrote it after his death. If Paul wrote it, he probably did so in the AD 60s, shortly before his execution.

● *Main characters:*
Paul, a travelling minister who started churches throughout the Roman Empire
Timothy, Paul's most devoted associate and the pastor of the church at Ephesus

● *Biggest scene:*
Paul warns Timothy against using religion as a way to get rich. 'If we have enough food and clothing, let us be content. But people who long to be rich fall into temptation and are trapped by many foolish and harmful desires that plunge them into ruin and destruction' (1 Timothy 6:8–9).

● *Most famous line:*
'The love of money is the root of all evil' (1 Timothy 6:10).

2 Timothy

● *In a paragraph:*
On the brink of execution, Paul writes what many believe is his last surviving letter – a deeply personal word to his closest friend, Timothy. All of Paul's associates have abandoned him, except Luke. Cold and in chains, perhaps in a Roman prison, Paul asks his friend of fifteen years or more to come. The journey to Rome from Ephesus, where Timothy is pastoring, is about 1,600 kilometres (1,000 miles) by sea and land. Perhaps fearing Timothy won't arrive in time, Paul writes tender words of advice and encouragement that sound like a father talking with his son for the last time. 'Work hard so God can approve you. Be a good worker, one who does not need to be ashamed and who correctly explains the word of truth' (2 Timothy 2:15).

● *Key point:*
'Do the work of telling the Good News, and complete all the duties of a servant of God' (2 Timothy 4:5).

● *Author, date:*
The apostle Paul wrote this letter from jail, probably in Rome, shortly before his execution in the AD 60s.

● *Main characters:*
Paul, an apostle and travelling minister facing execution
Timothy, Paul's beloved associate who is like a son to him

● *Biggest scene:*
Sitting in jail, awaiting imminent execution, Paul writes to his closest friend: 'Now the time has come for me to die... a crown will be given to me for pleasing the Lord' (2 Timothy 4:6, 8).

● *Most famous line:*
'I have fought a good fight, I have finished the race, and I have remained faithful' (2 Timothy 4:7).

Titus

● *In a paragraph:*
The apostle Paul writes this letter of pastoral advice to Titus, an associate to whom Paul has assigned the job of organizing churches on the island of Crete. Paul gives much the same advice to Titus as he did to Timothy, pastoring in Ephesus, including qualifications to look for in church leaders and what to teach different groups in the church. For example, Paul says young men need wisdom, young women need to devote themselves to their family, and elderly women need to avoid criticizing people. Paul also advises Titus not to get into verbal duels with intruders who are trying to lure Christians into heresy. Instead, Titus is to 'stay away from those who have foolish arguments' (Titus 3:9).

● *Key point:*
'Teach them [the people of Crete] to know the truth that shows them how to live godly lives' (Titus 1:1).

● *Author, date:*
Paul, perhaps in the AD 60s, shortly before his execution

● *Main characters:*
Paul, a travelling minister who started churches throughout
the Roman Empire
Titus, one of Paul's associates and the missionary Paul appointed
to organize churches in Crete

● *Biggest scene:*
Titus, searching for pastors to lead churches on the island of
Crete, is looking for men who are well-respected, faithful
husbands, and good fathers. Any person chosen 'must not be
arrogant or quick-tempered; he must not be a heavy drinker,
violent, or greedy for money. He must enjoy having guests in his
home and must love all that is good' (Titus 1:7–8).

● *Most famous line:*
'The grace of God that brings salvation has appeared to all men'
(Titus 2:11).

Philemon

● *In a paragraph:*
Paul convinces runaway slave Onesimus to return to his master,
taking with him this short letter from Paul to help protect him.
The slave's master is Philemon, in whose home the Christians
of Colosse meet for worship. Paul, widely considered to be the
leader of the Christian movement throughout the Roman
Empire as he started many of its churches, writes as if he is
Philemon's boss – a bit like a bishop to a parish minister. Paul
asks Philemon for a favour: 'Show kindness to Onesimus. I
think of him as my own son because he became a believer as a
result of my ministry here in prison' (Philemon 10). Paul says
he wanted to keep Onesimus as an assistant, but not without
Philemon's consent – a hint that Paul would welcome
Onesimus' freedom. Paul vows to visit soon, and to pay for
anything Onesimus stole or damaged during his escape.

● *Key point:*
Paul is asking a Christian slave owner to welcome home a runaway slave. And in several not-so-subtle hints, Paul seems to be asking for the slave's freedom.

● *Author, date:*
The apostle Paul writing from jail, perhaps during his two years of house arrest in Rome, which began around AD 60

● *Main characters:*
Paul, a travelling minister who started churches throughout the Roman Empire
Philemon, a church leader and slave owner
Onesimus, a slave who ran away from Philemon

● *Biggest scene:*
Slave owner Philemon is told to prepare a guest room for Paul, who vows to come for a visit – obviously to make sure Philemon has done everything Paul asked him to do. And the very least he asked for was kindness towards the runaway slave Onesimus. To increase the pressure on Philemon, Paul adds: 'I am confident as I write this letter that you will do what I ask and even more!' (Philemon 21).

● *Most famous line:*
'He is no longer just a slave; he is a beloved brother' (Philemon 16).

Hebrews

● *In a paragraph:*
Several decades after Jesus – perhaps when the Romans have started feeding Christians to the lions – many Jews who converted to Christianity begin to abandon it. They return to the synagogue, apparently disillusioned and tired of the constant persecution they're facing as Christians. An anonymous church leader writes this brilliant essay explaining why Jews should stay in the church. He argues that Jesus, as God's Son, is a better leader than any of the Jewish heroes of old – including Moses and Abraham. Jesus is a better intercessor than the Jewish priests because Jesus never sinned.

Jesus is a better sacrifice than even the best livestock because Jesus is perfect. And Jesus' arrival as the long-awaited messiah renders the old covenant between God and humanity obsolete. That means there's nothing for the Jews to go back to.

● *Key point:*
Jewish laws are out of date. 'When God speaks of a new covenant, it means he has made the first one obsolete. It is now out of date and ready to be put aside' (Hebrews 8:13).

● *Author, date:*
Unknown. Some early church leaders said Paul wrote it. But the writing style is different from Paul's, and the writer implies he had never met Jesus, though Paul insists otherwise (compare Hebrew 2:3 with Acts 9:5–6). Other contenders include Barnabas, Apollos, Luke and Silas.

● *Main character:*
Jesus, God's Son, who made the Jewish covenant obsolete and set up a new agreement between God and humanity

Biggest scene:
God makes a promise some 600 years before Jesus: 'The day will come, says the Lord, when I will make a new covenant with the people of Israel' (Hebrews 8:8). At the Last Supper Jesus raised a cup of wine and said, 'This wine is the token of God's new covenant to save you – an agreement sealed with the blood I will pour out for you' (Luke 22:20).

● *Most famous line:*
'Jesus Christ is the same yesterday, today, and forever' (Hebrews 13:8).

James

● *In a paragraph:*
Like the Old Testament book of Proverbs, James is a collection of wise sayings on many topics – all of which deal with how to live as God's people. Here is a sample:

'Be quick to listen, slow to speak, and slow to get angry' (James 1:19).

Bedouin beggars in 1899. James encouraged Christians to practice their religion by helping people in need.

'If you claim to be religious but don't control your tongue, you are just fooling yourself, and your religion is worthless' (James 1:26).

'If you pay special attention to the rich, you are committing a sin' (James 2:9).

'I can't see your faith if you don't have good deeds, but I will show you my faith through my good deeds' (James 2:18).

'When you bow down before the Lord and admit your dependence on him, he will lift you up and give you honour' (James 4:10).

● *Key point:*
If you're a Christian, people will know it by the way you live. 'Faith that does not result in good deeds is useless' (James 2:20).

● *Author, date:*
'This letter is from James, a slave of God and of the Lord Jesus

Christ' (James 1:1). This particular James may have been Jesus' oldest brother, who led the Jerusalem church until he was executed in the late AD 60s.

● *Main character:*
James, a church leader who wrote this book and who may have been the brother of Jesus

● *Biggest scene:*
Like a spark that sets fire to a forest, the tiny human tongue 'can turn the entire course of your life into a blazing flame of destruction, for it is set on fire by hell itself' (James 3:6).

● *Most famous line:*
'Resist the Devil, and he will flee from you. Draw close to God, and God will draw close to you' (James 4:7–8).

1 Peter

● *In a paragraph:*
Christians throughout what is now Turkey are facing some kind of orchestrated persecution. This may be the beginning of the Roman persecution led by the Emperor Nero, after he blamed Christians for starting the fire that destroyed two-thirds of Rome in AD 64. Calling this a test of faith, Peter assures Christians, 'if your faith remains strong after being tried... Your reward for trusting [God] will be the salvation of your souls' (1 Peter 1:7, 9). Peter advises them to submit to the authorities – especially the emperor – but to live godly lives, hold onto the faith, and be prepared to humbly explain their beliefs when asked about them.

● *Key point:*
'If you suffer for doing what is right, God will reward you for it' (1 Peter 3:14).

Pope Peter

Roman Catholics teach that Peter was the first pope – the top church official. They say Jesus gave him authority to act on behalf of God: 'I will give you the keys of the kingdom of heaven; the things you don't allow on earth will be the things that God does not allow, and the things you allow on earth will be the things that God allows' (Matthew 16:19).

Other Christians say that Jesus was simply putting Peter in charge of the ministry ahead, for the immediate future. Acts reports that after Jesus left, it was Peter who took charge by preaching a sermon that launched the Christian movement. Later, however, Peter became just one of many leaders, including James who took the helm of the Jerusalem church and Paul who led the missionary efforts abroad.

● *Author, date:*
The apostle Peter, 'with the help of Silas' (1 Peter 5:12). He may have written it in the AD mid-60s, shortly before the Romans executed him.

● *Main character:*
Peter, leader of Jesus' disciples and one of the key leaders of the early Christian movement

● *Biggest scene:*
Jesus hangs dying on a cross – a powerful image Peter invokes to inspire Christians as they suffer. 'Since Christ suffered physical pain, you must arm yourselves with the same attitude he had, and be ready to suffer, too' (1 Peter 4:1). Those who share his suffering, even to the point of death, 'will have the wonderful joy of sharing his glory when it is displayed to all the world' (1 Peter 4:13).

● *Most famous line:*
'Give all your worries and cares to God, for he cares about what happens to you' (1 Peter 5:7).

2 Peter

● *In a paragraph:*
'The Lord Jesus Christ has shown me that my days here on earth are numbered and I am soon to die' (2 Peter 1:14). In what was probably Peter's last open letter to Christians scattered in churches throughout Turkey, he warns of false teachers who will try to lure them away from Christian teachings. And he assures those who are eager for Jesus to come back that the Lord will return when the time is right. 'The Lord isn't really being slow about his promise to return, as some people think. No, he is being patient for your sake. He does not want anyone to perish, so he is giving more time for everyone to repent' (2 Peter 3:9). As Christians wait for Jesus, Peter urges them to live pure lives, at peace with God.

● *Key point:*
Don't let yourself be misled by evil people posing as ministers.
'Their destruction is on the way' (2 Peter 2:3).

● *Author, date:*
'This letter is from Simon Peter, a slave and apostle of Jesus Christ' (2 Peter 1:1). If Peter wrote this letter, he did so shortly before the Romans executed him in the AD mid-60s. Some scholars suspect the writer may have been a student of Peter's writing on behalf of his mentor. That's because the writer classifies Paul's writings as 'Scripture' (2 Peter 3:16).

● *Main character:*
Peter, leader of Jesus' disciples and one of the leaders of the Christian church

● *Biggest scene:*
False teachers posing as Christians worm their way into the church for one reason only: 'your money' (2 Peter 2:3). They swindle Christians not only out of their money but out of their faith, too. 'They make a game of luring unstable people into sin' (2 Peter 2:14). And they openly commit sins as blatant as adultery, insisting there's nothing wrong with it.

● *Most famous line:*
'A day is like a thousand years to the Lord, and a thousand years is like a day' (2 Peter 3:8).

1 John

● *In a paragraph:*
An unidentified Christian leader, presumed to be Jesus' disciple, John, writes this open letter to churches being split apart by 'antichrists' – enemies of Christ. John seems to be referring to a splinter group that will eventually blossom into a heresy called Gnosticism, from the Greek word for knowledge: *gnosis*. They teach that secret knowledge is what saves us, not Jesus. These people have strange ideas about Jesus. They presume that everything physical is evil, so they conclude that Jesus didn't come to earth as a human. He just looked human. And he only seemed to die. John warns Christians away from distorted teachings like this, and points Christians back to the message they heard from the beginning: Jesus came in human form and died to save people from their sins. John also reminds

Christians of another basic teaching: 'We should love one another' (1 John 3:11).

● *Key point:*

'I have written these things to you because you need to be aware of those who want to lead you astray. But you have received the Holy Spirit, and he lives within you, so you don't need anyone to teach you what is true. For the Spirit teaches you all things, and what he teaches is true – it is not a lie. So continue in what he has taught you, and continue to live in Christ' (1 John 2:26–27).

● *Author, date:*

The writer never identifies himself, but the writing style is so much like the Gospel of John, along with 2 and 3 John, that most experts agree one person wrote them all. Church leaders as early as the AD 100s said John, Jesus' disciple, wrote these books. They were probably written in the AD 90s.

● *Main character:*

Jesus, God's Son who came to earth as a human to die for the sins of humanity, save them from their sins, and prepare an eternal home for them in heaven

● *Biggest scene:*

'Antichrists' form a splinter movement that breaks off from the Christian church, taking many of its members with it. This group puts a new and outlandish slant on the Christian faith. Because it's similar to authentic Christianity, it's especially deceptive. But John cuts through the deception: 'When they left us, it proved that they do not belong with us' (1 John 2:19).

● *Most famous line:*

'If we confess our sins to him [Jesus], he is faithful and just to forgive us and to cleanse us from every wrong' (1 John 1:9).

2 John

● *In a paragraph:*

In a short note of thirteen verses, which reads like a P.S. to 1 John, the writer highlights two key points:

Love one another.

Stay away from false teachers, 'antichrists' who can lure you away from your eternal reward. Don't even welcome them into your house.

● *Key point:*
'We should love one another. This is not a new commandment, but one we had from the beginning' (2 John 5).

● *Author, date:*
The writer identifies himself only as a church leader – an elder. But the writing style is so much like the Gospel of John, along with 1 and 3 John, that most experts agree one person wrote them all, probably in the AD 90s.

● *Main characters:*
The elder, presumably the apostle John
The chosen lady, which is the church

● *Biggest scene:*
A person claiming to be a Christian comes into the church and starts teaching bizarre ideas that clash with teachings of Jesus' disciples. 'Anyone who encourages him becomes a partner in his evil work' (2 John 11).

● *Most famous line:*
'Love one another' (2 John 5).

3 John

● *In a paragraph:*
This is a short, personal note to a church leader named Gaius. The writer – presumably the apostle John – commends him for showing hospitality to travelling Christian teachers who arrive in town. But John condemns a power-hungry minister who refuses to welcome the visiting teachers and excommunicates church members who do. 'Remember,' John writes, 'those who do evil prove that they do not know God' (3 John 11).

● *Key point:*
Churches should support ministers who travel. 'They are travelling for the Lord and accept nothing from those who are

not Christians. So we ourselves should support them so that we may become partners with them for the truth' (3 John 7–8).

● *Author, date:*
See 1 and 2 John.

● *Main characters:*
The elder, presumably the apostle John
Gaius, a church leader who shows kindness to Christians who are passing through
Diotrephes, a tyrannical minister who abuses his authority by excommunicating church members who disagree with him

● *Biggest scene:*
A showdown is coming. A maverick minister who clings to his power by kicking people who disagree with him out of the church will have to face charges that an elder – probably the apostle John – will level against him when John comes to town.

● *Most famous line:*
'Do not imitate what is evil but what is good' (3 John 11).

Jude

● *In a paragraph:*
Jude writes an open letter to Christians everywhere, warning them about a new heresy which is infiltrating the church. 'Some godless people have wormed their way in among you, saying that God's forgiveness allows us to live immoral lives' (Jude 4). Jude says they are dead wrong, and that history is littered with corpses to prove it. God sent invaders to wipe out the entire Jewish nation for their persistent sin. God destroyed the cities of Sodom and Gomorrah, and he even punished disobedient angels. 'You, dear friends, must continue to build your lives on the foundation of your holy faith' Jude writes. 'Live in such a way that God's love can bless you as you wait for the eternal life that our Lord Jesus Christ in his mercy is going to give you' (Jude 20–21).

● *Key point:*
God's forgiveness is no excuse for continuing to sin. God punishes sinful people – as history proves.

● *Author, date:*
'Jude, a servant of Jesus Christ and a brother of James' (Jude 1). Jude is a nickname for Judas. James and Judas were brothers of Jesus, and early church leaders said that the Jude who wrote this short letter was the brother of Jesus. Jude probably wrote this letter sometime in the middle of the first Christian century.

● *Main character:*
Jude, author of this letter and probably a brother of Jesus

● *Biggest scene:*
Sodom and Gomorrah – twin cities obsessed with sexual immorality and perversion – are seared off the planet in a fireball. 'They serve as an example of those who suffer the punishment of eternal fire' (Jude 7).

● *Most famous line:*
'To the only God our Savior be glory, majesty, power and authority, through Jesus Christ our Lord, before all ages, now and forevermore! Amen' (Jude 25).

Mark of the beast

'You need wisdom to understand the number of the beast! But if you are smart enough, you can figure this out. Its number is six hundred sixty-six, and it stands for a person' (Revelation 13:18).

Many Bible experts say the beast was Nero, the Roman emperor who launched 300 years of Christian persecution. Greek letters had number equivalents, something like A=1, B=2. Nero's name and title – Caesar Nero – make a total of 666.

Revelation

● *In a paragraph:*
Exiled to Patmos, a small island off the coast of Turkey, John sees incredible visions about the end of human history and the beginning of eternal life in heaven with God. He sees:
Horsemen of the apocalypse, symbolizing war, famine and disease.
Martyred Christians.
Cataclysmic disasters: earthquakes, hail, fire. 'A great flaming

What is hell like?

Bible experts can't agree.

Even Jesus painted conflicting images. Sometimes he spoke of hell as a place of fire, but at other times he called it a place of darkness – though fire displaces darkness (compare Matthew 5:22 with 8:12).

Scholars offer these theories about what hell is like:

- A real place where sinners suffer forever in fire

- A symbol of eternal separation from God

- A symbol of annihilation. Just as fire destroys something forever, God will destroy sinners forever. It's the destruction, not the torment, that will last forever

- Not a place of punishment, but of reflection. God is loving, and he will keep sinners alive forever – not to punish them, but to give them a chance to repent

star fell out of the sky, burning like a torch' (Revelation 8:10).

A river of blood as high as a horse's bridle and flowing 300 kilometres (180 miles).

Satan defeated and thrown into a 'lake of fire' (Revelation 20:10).

Judgment Day, with all people judged according to how they lived. 'Anyone whose name was not found recorded in the Book of Life was thrown into the lake of fire' (Revelation 20:15).

Life in heaven. 'There will be no more death or sorrow or crying or pain. For the old world and its evils are gone forever' (Revelation 21:4).

- *Key point:*

God and goodness defeat Satan and evil. The humans who sided with God will live with him forever.

- *Author, date:*

The writer identifies himself only as 'God's servant, John'. Church leaders in the AD 100s said it was the apostle John, who is presumed to have also written the Gospel of John, along with 1, 2 and 3 John. Most Bible experts say John wrote this book during the Roman persecution of Christians in the AD 90s.

- *Main characters:*

John, the author of this book and probably one of Jesus' closest disciples

Jesus, the Son of God who returns to earth to judge humanity and to take Christians to heaven

- *Biggest scene:*

John looks into heaven and describes the indescribable using the closest earthly comparisons he can think of. Gates of pearl, walls of precious jasper, and a city of crystal clear gold – with everything illuminated by God's shimmering glory. 'Nothing evil will be allowed to enter' (Revelation 21:27).

● *Most famous line:*

'I am the Alpha and the Omega – the beginning and the end' (Revelation 1:8).

Patmos island, off the coast of Turkey. Exiled here, John wrote the book of Revelation.

What is heaven like?

Don't expect pearly gates, jasper walls, and a city paved in gold, most Bible experts say.

Though John the Revelator said heaven had all of these, Bible scholars say John was simply drawing from earth's most precious objects to describe something that's beyond earthly comparison.

For example, John said heaven is in the form of a cube measuring 2,250 kilometres (1,400 miles) in every direction. A cube symbolized holiness because the most sacred room in the Jewish temple was a cube. It held Israel's most sacred object, the Ark of the Covenant, a chest that contained the Ten Commandments. This room measured only nine cubic meters (thirty cubic feet). So the portrait of heaven as a massive cube could symbolize that heaven is unimaginably more holy than the holiest spot on earth.

Whatever heaven is like, it is God's presence that makes it heaven. 'The home of God is now among his people! He will live with them, and they will be his people' (Revelation 21:3).

THE ROMAN EMPIRE IN THE TIME OF CHRIST

Emperor Augustus, who ruled Rome when Jesus was born, brought peace, prosperity and stability to the Roman Empire. By the time of his death in AD 14, Roman territory and allied nations completely engulfed the Mediterranean world.

ATLANTIC
OCEAN

BRITANNIA

GERMANIA INFERIOR

LUGDUNENSIS   BELGICA

GERMANIA SUPERIOR   RAET

AQUITANIA

NARBONENSIS   ALPES POENINA

LUSITANIA   TARRACONENSIS   ALPES COTTIAE   ALPES MARITIMAE

CORSICA

BAETICA   SARDINIA

MAURETANIA   Carthage

AFRICA

☐ Roman Empire in 14 AD
☐ Client state
--- Boundary of province
— Roman Empire at its greatest extent in 116 AD
— Roman road

0   250   500 km
0   100   200   300 miles

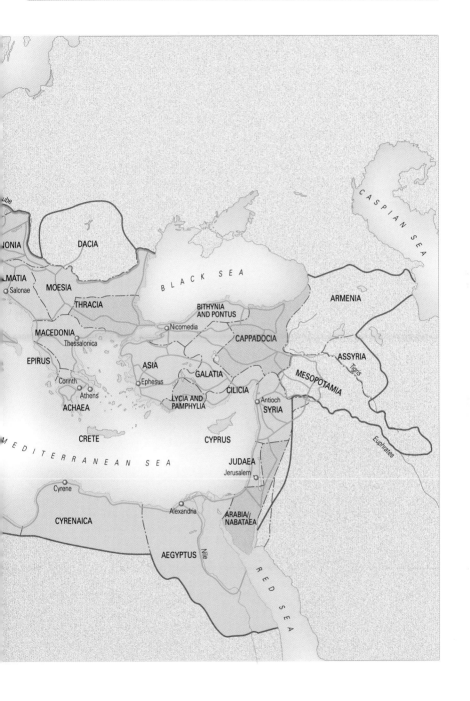

Text acknowledgments

pp. 7, 10, 12, 15–22, 24, 29, 34–36, 38–60, 64–66, 68–72, 74–81, 84–85, 87–89, 92–93, 95, 97, 99–100, 102–123 Scripture quotations are taken from the *Holy Bible, New Living Translation*, copyright © 1996. Used by permission of Tyndale House Publishers, Inc., Wheaton, Illinois 60189. All rights reserved.

pp. 14, 15–16 Scripture taken from *The Message*. Copyright © 1993, 1994, 1995, 1996, 2000, 2001, 2002. Used by permission of NavPress Publishing Group.

pp. 39, 55, 58, 62, 65, 69, 76, 97, 106, 107, 111, 121 Scripture quotations taken from the *Holy Bible, New International Version*, copyright © 1973, 1978, 1984 International Bible Society. Used by permission of Zondervan and Hodder & Stoughton Limited. All rights reserved. The 'NIV' and 'New International Version' trademarks are registered in the United States Patent and Trademark Office by International Bible Society. Use of either trademark requires the permission of International Bible Society. UK trademark number 1448790.

pp. 57-58 Extracts taken from the *New King James Version* copyright © 1982, 1979 by Thomas Nelson, Inc.

pp. 65, 91, 109 Extracts from the *Authorized Version* of the Bible (*The King James Bible*), the rights in which are vested in the Crown, are reproduced by permission of the Crown's Patentee, Cambridge University Press.

Picture acknowledgments

Picture research by Zooid Pictures Limited.

AKG – Images: pp. 17, 33, 48, 50, 61, 73.

Bridgeman Art Library: p. 94.

Corbis UK Ltd.: pp. 19, 35, 41, 67, 85, 86, 104, 123.

David Alexander: pp. 38, 42, 45, 56, 72, 91, 98.

Digital Vision: p. 11.

John Rylands University Library of Manchester: p. 13.

Library of Congress: p. 114 (Prints & Photographs Division).

Lion Hudson: p. 23 (David Townsend).

Reuters: p. 36 (Aladin Abdel Naby).

Three's Company: pp. 37, 47 (Richard Scott, copyright © Lion Hudson plc/Tim Dowley & Peter Wyart trading as Three's Company); 40, 96, 124–125 (Hardlines, copyright © Lion Hudson plc/Tim Dowley & Peter Wyart trading as Three's Company).

Zev Radovan, Jerusalem: pp. 16, 26, 53, 62, 64, 89.